The Perpetual Pivot

The Perpetual Pivot

Ministry in the Pandemic and Beyond

SUSAN CARTMELL
and PEGGY O'CONNOR

WIPF & STOCK · Eugene, Oregon

THE PERPETUAL PIVOT
Ministry in the Pandemic and Beyond

Copyright © 2023 Susan Cartmell and Peggy O'Connor. All rights reserved. Except for brief quotations in critical publications or reviews, no part of this book may be reproduced in any manner without prior written permission from the publisher. Write: Permissions, Wipf and Stock Publishers, 199 W. 8th Ave., Suite 3, Eugene, OR 97401.

Wipf & Stock
An Imprint of Wipf and Stock Publishers
199 W. 8th Ave., Suite 3
Eugene, OR 97401

www.wipfandstock.com

PAPERBACK ISBN: 978-1-6667-7167-1
HARDCOVER ISBN: 978-1-6667-7168-8
EBOOK ISBN: 978-1-6667-7169-5

VERSION NUMBER 12/05/23

Contents

Introduction | vii

1. Unsung Heroes | 1
2. The Flywheel of Worship and How it Changed | 17
3. What about the People? | 38
4. Community Ministry Explodes | 47
5. Crisis Leadership: New Authority or Mutiny on the Bounty? | 61
6. The Toll on Clergy | 75
7. What Does This Mean for the Future? | 93

Who We Are | 119
Acknowledgements | 121
List of Clergy Interviewed & The Questions | 123
Bibliography | 129

Introduction

THE WEEK OF MARCH 8, 2020, churches changed forever, and we are still trying to identify and understand what those changes mean.

It happened in plain sight, but many people missed it. It was a crisis for organized religion and for religious leaders from every faith. Though religious institutions have always formed one of the foundations of our culture, in the face of the public health crisis posed by the recent COVID-19 pandemic, with its tsunami of upheaval, few people besides religious leaders noticed the profound impact that this pandemic was having on our faith communities.

Something unusual happened in American churches and synagogues when the COVID pandemic hit in spring 2020. Across denominations and even faith traditions, many clergy suddenly had to lead their congregations in vast new ways. While the toll the crisis took on frontline workers grabbed headline after headline, the story of clergy has largely flown under the radar. Pastors and rabbis navigated this new territory quietly, humbly, and without much fanfare. It is a story we believe needs to be told.

We come to this topic with our own stories. As pastors in the United Church of Christ (UCC), between us we have served ten different congregations. In March 2020 Susan was a pastor serving a church on Cape Cod, and Peggy was in between interim assignments. As the crisis unfolded, month after uncertain month, we worked together to create new ways to lead the church Susan served. As we faced the challenges of church leadership, we came

INTRODUCTION

to believe that religious communities were in the throes of enormous change. We wanted to learn from other pastors about how they had fared, what challenges they had faced, and what they had learned. With that goal in mind, we offered a series of workshops on Zoom for clergy in the UCC's Southern New England Conference, comprising churches in Massachusetts, Rhode Island, and Connecticut. What happened in those gatherings surprised us.

We felt certain that the pandemic was beginning to transform religious life, but we had no idea how profound those changes were. Every clergy person in those workshops was worried, since the pandemic hit at a time when faith communities were already struggling with declining membership and shrinking budgets. For years, they had been trying to lead congregations in an atmosphere of uncertainty, when more and more sports and children's activities were crowding into Sunday morning schedules. However, at each workshop we were amazed by the stories clergy shared with us of how they had faced the pandemic—their struggles, obstacles, disappointments, and exhaustion. We heard stories about courage, self-reflection and inventiveness. We often lost track of time because it was clear to us that people needed to share their experiences, to find some affirmation for their various feelings and to feel heard. Over and over, we were also intrigued by the new questions they were asking about their profession, their call, and how to lead effectively. These conversations highlighted questions we all began to ask in the pandemic, questions about the future of the church generally as we move forward from this crisis. These workshops piqued our curiosity about what was happening to our profession and to religious communities in our society. We wanted to know more about how American churches had fared in the pandemic and how their leaders might be re-imagining the profession and this work of leading congregations. We wanted to talk to faith leaders about their questions now, as well as their plans, hopes, and fears for the future of the Church and for ministry itself. And so, the Post-Pandemic Church Project was born; at least that is what we called it then.

Introduction

We designed a set of questions for hour-long interviews and set a goal of talking to fifty clergy from different denominations and faith traditions. We met with them either in person or on Zoom. At first, we worried that we would not meet our goal, but we soon discovered that finding people to talk to was not a problem. In the end we spoke to fifty-three clergy. Some had even sought us out, and many thanked us for the chance to process this extraordinary experience. We heard unique stories with many resonant features. The sampling is diverse geographically, and few of the clergy knew one another.

Throughout this project our abiding interest has been with clergy as people. We sought to collect the stories of their experiences during the height of the COVID-19 pandemic, as they remembered what happened to them and to their churches. In many instances these clergy described poor behavior by members of their congregations and their deep disappointment at the lack of help or support they thought they received from the officials in their denominations or judicatories. We did not follow up with any denominational staff or with church members, as it would have been beyond the scope of this project. Our desire was to learn about and then to honor the profound experiences of the clergy, as they remembered them, and to tell their stories.

We started speaking to church leaders in August 2021 and held the last interview in May 2023. The pool of clergy came from six different Protestant denominations—Disciples of Christ (3), Evangelical Lutheran Church in America (2), Episcopalian Church (2), Friends-Quaker (1), United Methodist Church (4), United Presbyterian Church in the USA (8), United Church of Christ (31), as well as one Orthodox rabbi and one Greek Orthodox priest. We spoke to people from Cape Cod to Alaska, from Florida to Southern California. The pastor with the largest church was senior minister of seven thousand congregants. The pastor from the smallest had twenty in her congregation. We were surprised by similarities in these interviews; apparently neither theology nor geography played a role in the experience of pastoring a church during the pandemic.

Introduction

For most of the pandemic and the writing time Susan served two churches, one on Cape Cod where she was a settled pastor when the pandemic began, and then one in Central Wisconsin where she was an interim pastor. Neither of us were neutral reporters as we listened to our colleagues and gathered this data. Our own experiences helped us appreciate what we were hearing, but we freely admit that our experiences brought their own bias. Our impressions of churches informed our questions and influenced how we interpreted what we heard. We came to this project with great empathy for the colleagues we spoke to, an empathy that grew with every story we heard. We hope our own experiences were an asset in the listening process, and where it felt appropriate, we have included some stories of our own.

This introduction lays out the format for this book and explains its themes and direction. In chapter 1 we begin with the question "What is unique about churches that made them especially vulnerable in the COVID-19 pandemic?" As we look at the pace of change that was required of religious leaders, and the unprecedented flexibility they needed, we conclude that COVID affected religious institutions in ways that took a greater toll on them than on other institutions, largely because faith communities bring people together in crowded spaces. Working often invisibly below the cultural radar, many clergy became the social glue for their communities in this crisis because they were relentless in their commitment to serve others. We suggest that their herculean effort may make them the unsung heroes of this pandemic.

Over the next three chapters we look at how the clergy accomplished this remarkable feat of leadership in the midst of this public health crisis. Faith communities provide three basic functions in our society. They lead worship, which we identify as the Priestly function. They occupy the role at the center of the congregation as counselor and caregiver for the sick or perplexed, which we identify as the Pastoral function. The third component of ministry involves the role of the Prophet, the one who addresses societal or community injustice. Good ministry involves all three components—effective worship leadership, compassionate

Introduction

caregiving, and the ability to cast a vision for what the world might look like when people live in light of the values of faith.

Chapter 2 examines the hurdles faith leaders had to face to fulfill the Priestly function and lead worship services in the pandemic. Fulfilling this basic function as worship leaders required clergy to reimagine where they gathered and how they led their services to pray and praise God. As the health crisis called into question traditional practices and patterns for leading services, faith leaders found creative ways to continue and designed new ways to congregate safely. Even with all the obstacles in their path, they remained faithful to their core responsibility to lead worship services. We explain how they did that.

The second basic responsibility for many faith leaders is visiting the sick in hospitals or nursing facilities. This Pastoral function includes counseling families in times of loss or grief, praying with the dying, celebrating a birth or baptism or bris. In this international health crisis, all familiar ways of pastoring were almost completely curtailed. When visitation was allowed, it was extremely limited. Chapter 3 examines the pastoral crisis posed by a pandemic where people were sick but unable to connect to a pastor or rabbi, even on their deathbeds. In a pandemic in which families had to face the death of a loved one stripped of the ability to visit or say "goodbye," many families discovered that customary visitation from a faith leader and even normal funeral rites were suspended or put on hold. The societal trauma brought on by the grief of such widespread loss and the ripple effects of these restrictions caused clergy to minister in new ways. Many invented creative ways to reach people and we'll discuss how they did it.

Chapter 4 recounts how clergy recognized the opportunity to become more Prophetic in this healthcare crisis. Many recognized wider societal needs in their communities and addressed them. Many responded to the racial inequity exposed by the pandemic and spoke eloquently from their bully pulpits online. Many created new ministries during the pandemic to reach out to wider circles of people and address the needs they saw for food, clothing, and even internet. One of our more surprising discoveries was that

INTRODUCTION

though clergy were stretched thin in so many ways, they found enormous energy to reach beyond the walls of their buildings in bold new endeavors that ultimately changed the mission and even the identity of their congregations.

In chapter 5, we discuss the new issues of authority laid bare in the pandemic as clergy stepped into increasingly prominent roles of leadership in their congregations and in the wider community. Like Moses, faith leaders found themselves in a wilderness without a map, so they had to summon all their authority to bring their people on this journey. As leadership patterns were thrown into disarray, they were forced to make changes in how they led their faith communities, but many paid a price for this creative leadership.

Chapter 6 looks at the toll of this crisis on the clergy. The challenges and creativity involved in redesigning how to run a faith community and reimagining their jobs took an enormous toll on many faith leaders. In chapter 6 we consider the fatigue and exhaustion that resulted. Pushed to their limit, many clergy experienced enormous stress doing their jobs. We talk about the cost of this experience and how COVID both depleted them and taught them some new ways to thrive.

In every interview we conducted, faith leaders raised questions about how the pandemic was changing American religious life. Chapter 7 discusses these fundamental questions about how religion itself has been altered by the pandemic experience. This COVID pandemic has prompted faith leaders to ask how to conduct worship services or lead meetings in an online world, how to continue to serve their flock pastorally, how to minister to a wider swathe of the community and address societal injustice. Many clergy also gave voice to new questions the pandemic raised about authority and leadership. We cannot answer most of their questions and won't try to. But these gleanings from the pandemic experience will shape our faith communities as we look to the future.

This is the story of how clergy faced the hardest professional adversity of their lifetimes and still served the spiritual needs of their people. It is a story of fortitude and of passion for this work.

Introduction

It is also a story of the deep wells of compassion that sustained their efforts to meet the needs of others in this crisis. It is a story of grinding fatigue and tremendous change in a short span of time.

Much attention was rightly focused on healthcare workers and what became known as "essential workers," but as we conducted these interviews, we recognized that the clergy have not generally been recognized as essential workers in any way that is commensurate with what they have done. We hope that this book will demonstrate their role in this moment of history and help to shine a light on the challenges they faced, the fortitude they found, the responsibility they felt, and the personal toll it took on them.

We are so very grateful to our clergy colleagues who lead congregations and who spent time explaining to us how this experience pushed them and changed the way they do this work they love. Again and again in these interviews we felt blessed to hear people reflect with such candor and wisdom. We endeavored to listen faithfully and honor their willingness to be vulnerable in hopes that we might all learn from each other and together be better able to shape the congregations that will rise like phoenixes from this experience.

"We cannot know we have no ownership over what is to come. The best we can do is map our moment scrupulously, to preserve the signposts that will lead to a place we'll never see. As curators, as historians, as citizens we are frequently reminded that the past is a foreign country. But so is the future."
—Jon Grinspan and Peter Manseau, Op-Ed in *New York Times*, January 6, 2022[1]

Susan Cartmell and Peggy O'Connor

---

1. Grinspan and Manseau, "It's 2086."

1

Unsung Heroes

"In thirty-five years of ministry my life's work has been to bring people together. Now I have to bring them together while keeping them apart."
—Rev. James Brewer-Calvert, Decatur, Georgia

In August 2021, seventeen months into the pandemic, we were at the Chautauqua United Church of Christ Society in Western New York State. The Society sits at the center of a two-thousand-acre campus where eight-thousand to ten thousand people gather weekly in the summer to attend lectures, worship services, and musical performances. Although folks were nervous that summer about how the pandemic would change things, the experience turned out to be remarkably similar to previous years.

Customarily, the United Church of Christ Society invites a different clergy person to be their chaplain every week. These chaplains serve guests at the UCC denominational houses as pastors for the week. As guests settled into these denominational houses for the third week of August, folks were relaxing into the relatively safe

The Perpetual Pivot

bubble that surrounded the grounds. Rev. Julie Peeples, a pastor from Greensboro, North Carolina, was the chaplain that week. She and her associate minister husband, Rev. Paul Davis, were found most days sitting in side-by-side rockers on the ample front porch listening to a lecture or a musical group in the nearby amphitheater. She had presided at the Sunday morning worship and was preparing to relax a little.

Then, on Tuesday of that week, Peebles received the email that every pastor feared in 2020 and 2021. A couple from their congregation had contracted COVID-19. The couple had attended worship the Sunday before, without knowing they were ill. Now, they were quite sick. Peeples and Davis sequestered themselves in their room and went into high gear. As they managed this crisis from six states away, they kept wondering if they should get in the car and drive all night to be there in person with their congregation. That impulse was driven by months of shepherding people through one challenge after another, and through all those months being physically present in the community was a compelling aspect of their successful leadership.

Initially they studied the video footage from the weekly worship service, trying to see where their sick parishioners had been sitting and who might have been exposed. From video footage, they determined that the congregation seemed safely distanced on that Sunday. Next, they wrote a letter to their 250 members, explaining the situation and repeating the safety precautions, careful to choose words that set a calm, reassuring, pastoral tone. Then, they called their sick parishioners to express their concern, to connect personally, and to pray with them over the phone. After that, they reviewed the state and county public health protocols for religious communities again. Next, they held Zoom meetings with church leaders to talk about the crisis, hear their ideas and design a response plan. Finally, they activated their congregation's phone tree to reach out to the widest swath of the congregation and collect questions and reactions. For hours, they huddled together as they worked. Those of us watching sympathized and understood the burden of responsibility that they felt as church leaders in this pandemic; we tried to give them space to do what they felt they needed to do.

After forty-eight hours, the crisis had shifted from high alert to a manageable sense of caution. The sick couple did not need to be hospitalized and Peeples and Davis remained at the Chautauqua Institute for the rest of the week so she could fulfill her duties as chaplain. These two had faced the nightmare so many clergy dreaded in those months of 2020–21 as they led congregations during the COVID-19 pandemic.

❖

The fateful weeks of March 2020 were a game changer for most religious leaders. The mysterious illness in Asia spread in isolated cases to the Pacific Northwest. Then came the news story about a choir rehearsal in Skagit County, Washington, that turned frightening when 86 percent of the people gathered there came down with COVID-19. Several died. As the term "super spreader" entered the lexicon, clergy in every state suddenly became fearful of replicating the Skagit County experience. Within days religious houses closed and locked their doors, something that no one could remember ever happening in their lifetimes, indeed in modern history. By the end of the month, most churches and synagogues were shuttered.

For centuries religious communities have been designed to bring people together. Indeed, one could argue that this is the main purpose of religious institutions—to foster communities where people gather to praise God, to minister to one another, and to reach out to those in need. At the center of most religious life are organized gatherings where people share rituals, food, healing circles, study groups, and outreach projects. Nearly all the activities in faith communities revolve around organized gatherings. Bringing people together in groups for intimate experiences of prayer, music, or study lies at the heart of religious life. When it suddenly became unsafe to gather, new restrictions undermined organized religion as we know it. To be fair, these restrictions that ultimately saved millions of lives also transformed all institutions in our society. However we will argue that none were more affected than religious communities, calling into question their *raison* d'être. The people most affected by these sudden restrictions were faith leaders, who had to rethink everything they knew about how to do their work.

Most clergy are adept at creating close encounters among people by leading worship experiences where people engage in sharing food, anointing with water or oil, and listening to choirs. However, the pandemic called all of these ways of gathering into question. Every one of these events was suddenly deemed dangerous. Here we had a profession that measured success by moments when people were crowded together in pews, passing the peace, or shaking hands with strangers. Almost overnight sharing food, holding hands, and singing with abandon was forbidden. Preaching to crowds or presiding at funerals or weddings were all off the table, and the intimacy that defined religious life was suspect. A profession of people skilled and committed at promoting the spiritual health of their flocks could not reach those very people. Religious leaders had to balance their need to gather people in proximate ways with their responsibility to protect their well-being. That was the trade-off that so often confounded the clergy. Most people we interviewed were initially overwhelmed and profoundly baffled by this dilemma. The crisis called for more creativity than ever before as they had to rethink everything they thought they knew about how to do their jobs.

Until this moment in time, most religious leaders assumed that the greatest challenge they faced was to pray with the dying, interpret a thorny passage of scripture or inspire people to make a difference in the world. That job description was weighty enough. But during the COVID pandemic, even clergy who knew how to lead beautiful worship experiences, moderate messy council meetings, or bring a sense of peace to someone's deathbed had no idea how to navigate what had once been such familiar ground.

The pandemic arrived like a hurricane flinging church leaders onto the rocky beaches of a whole new terrain. To be sure, the COVID pandemic surged throughout our society, with a ferocious rearrangement of all ordered life, but clergy had an especially hard adjustment. Everything they knew about how to do their jobs and lead their congregations had to be reexamined.

For some, the frustrations became paramount. Barna Research[1] reported clergy burnout was a direct result of the pandemic. This data found that 42 percent of faith leaders seriously considered leaving full-time ministry. Even among those who had not considered quitting, 34 percent complained of unusual pressure and stress in trying to do their jobs. Running through our interviews was the prevailing complaint of fatigue that would not dissipate and stress that endured long after things started to return to normal. Everyone we spoke to had to reinvent their jobs. From worship to administration, from visiting the homebound to teaching youth—absolutely everything had to be rethought. Clergy rose to the occasion, but it was not easy. What they described was a process of building a plane while they were flying it and not knowing where they were going.

Though many gave voice to the stress they knew and the adversity they had faced, they also described a surge of creativity that we found impressive for its scope and impact. Clergy everywhere from large campuses to community chapels, from Cape Cod to California, met obstacles and found work-arounds. They redesigned worship services, reached out to the sick, and connected with strangers in need with astonishing speed. They reinvented themselves, their jobs, and the way they led their churches.

Faith leaders' jobs can be shrouded in mystery when life is uneventful, so it is easy to miss the lengths to which they went during the pandemic to keep things going. As we listened to the men and women who led faith communities during the pandemic, we often marveled at their resilience and their determination to persevere precisely when physically gathering, in person, was impossible. How did they do this? By being more flexible than ever before and by pivoting, not once but over and over.

---

1. Read more about Barna's research at this site: https://www.barna.com/research/pastors-quitting-ministry/ Barna began tracking these trends in 2021, when 38% of clergy were considering leaving the profession, but the trend has continued to rise.

CAUGHT IN DISBELIEF

In Boston's Back Bay, the Emmanuel Church had been planning for months to celebrate the rector's tenth anniversary. The congregation was proud to have called their first female rector and eager to recognize her decade of leadership. A formal dinner was scheduled for March 14, 2020, with a catered meal for one hundred and fifty people in the church hall. The rector, Rev. Pamela Werntz, recalled how they feted her with poems and songs. A vestry member read a special declaration from Mayor Marty Walsh. No one thought to mask that night. As a precautionary nod to the pandemic, they used tongs to serve the food but gave no thought to the fact the musicians for the evening had recently attended the Biogen Convention event in Boston. They did not know it at the time but that conference was an East Coast super spreader event, later seen as the original signal that the pandemic was indeed quite dangerous in New England. Blissfully ignorant of the danger, the dinner went off without a hitch, and no one got sick. But things might have been very different on the cusp of the COVID-19 shutdown.

When the pandemic hit, clergy like Werntz were blindsided. No one had a crystal ball, and most clergy assumed the early pandemic restrictions would be short-term. Many recalled how clueless they had been in the early days. One pastor served communion according to his church's usual custom, with a common, shared cup. Still another pastor hugged dozens of families at a funeral. Someone else played the friendly host at the local Cub Scout Pinewood Derby, mingling with crowds in the church hall. Another pastor in New England reported her sanctuary was packed that March when parishioners returned from Florida fearful of COVID there, but they thought nothing of crowding into their Vermont chapel, which felt like a safe haven.

❧

Rev. Nicole Shaw from Angola, Indiana, was scheduled to officiate at a family wedding on March 15 in Connecticut. While she was driving east with her husband and four children on March 12 she could see and feel the changes in each state as the country adjusted to the news of COVID's approach. From the car, she consulted with church leaders and changed her home worship to a virtual event, but the wedding went as planned. There were no masks but they had hand sanitizers available. Driving home after the ceremony, what she saw in other states convinced her this was serious.

Looking back, many people we spoke to laughed at their own incomprehension in those early days. But most clergy were not eager to curtail their activities. So, they continued serving in their public capacity until they could no longer avoid recognizing the changes all around them. Another pastor could not deny that the highways were bare and streets devoid of people. She told us that this was the first time the reality of this public health crisis began to set in. Her incredulity was representative of the clergy we spoke to. Somehow this discovery did not surprise us. Faith leaders can get immersed in their duties, often marching to their own drum. While not unaware of what is going on around them, there was a level of denial for many especially as they began to comprehend the extent of the changes that lay ahead.

When most churches closed their doors in March 2020, it was anathema for faith leaders who pride themselves on staying open in every season and in all kinds of weather; it took ecclesiastical directives to prompt the closures. Most of the clergy we spoke to took their cues from bishops, presbytery, and conference executives and synod leaders; others relied on advice from governors or the Center for Disease Control. Many clergy admitted that this was such unexplored territory they were grateful to allow ecclesiastical authorities or public health officials to make these initial controversial decisions.

For Christians who closed their churches that spring, the decision came during the season of Lent, a holy season of abstinence and sacrifice. This coincidence was not lost on pastors. But the general expectation was that the clergy could "power through" this crisis and be back in the pulpit by Easter, just shy of one month later. Several reflected ruefully that the shutdown accentuated the penitence of Lent, with its season of solitude and time for reflection. Rev. Beth Gedert, of Delaware, OH, captured the feeling when she said, "I thought this would be the Lentiest Lent I ever Lented." Soon, it would become clear that the COVID pandemic was much more significant than the impetus for a stricter observance of Lent. There were many challenges ahead that no one could anticipate.

HUGE SENSE OF RESPONSIBILITY

Clergy operate in their faith communities with a unique sense of responsibility and role as guardians of the welfare of their congregations. When they plan programs, worship services, or a visit to someone's home, they consider the educational, spiritual and emotional needs of their flock. The pandemic brought a brand new unwieldy calculus for most faith leaders as they struggled to figure out how best to serve the needs of their people. On one hand, they knew isolation and loneliness could take a toll on the congregation. On the other hand, they feared that encouraging folks to gather could be dangerous especially as many congregations are weighted toward the elderly who were far more susceptible to contracting the disease. On one hand, they knew people relied on one another for emotional support. On the other hand, it was hard to imagine how to create a community with these public health constraints. So clergy were always weighing how to keep people safe, and at the same time, supported spiritually. They worked hard to creatively maintain the balance between safety and connection. They became experts at navigating the tangle of local, state, and national public health guidelines.

Two trends emerged. As they faced all these new challenges many clergy reported a heady sense that they were needed and their skills were vital in the crisis. They believed that their people were relying on them at this moment and that God had called them to leadership for just this time. While acknowledging that they never felt so needed, they also felt a demand to work harder than ever before. While invigorated by a new sense of purpose, they were also driven to excel. Most agreed that they never worked so hard in their careers. One said, "There was no time to stop, and yet I never knew where I stood." It was like a race without a finish line, or like a bad dream in which the finish line kept receding. The biggest challenge was that the demands kept changing. No sooner had they solved one problem but another came bearing down, with urgency. But as soon as they settled into the next pattern, they had to pivot again.

In Decatur, Georgia, Rev. James Brewer-Calvert said, "I have been the senior pastor of this church since 1998. I'm patient and this is a long-term pastorate. It took us eighteen years to embrace the Open and Affirming Program, but in the pandemic we had to change everything in seven days. Now it's a challenge to keep up my level of energy and stay positive while living in this diaspora. It's been hard to keep positive, to keep saying that the church can do this with God, week after week for so many months. It's taking all my training and experience to stay on this course."

On top of the policies and strategies clergy had to devise to care for their people in such an unusual crisis, the society was also in the grips of a widespread trauma that affected everyone. Therapist and pastor Rev. Fritz Fowler from Lansdale, Pennsylvania, viewed this moment in history through a psychological lens. "Faith communities were trying to process the trauma in this pandemic and the power it has had over us, all while struggling to name this trauma and how it was affecting everyone, including themselves." To lead people in that kind of environment required both adaptability and optimism. Without a certain amount of "innate positivity," Fowler said, religious leaders would become overwhelmed.

Most church leaders expanded their roles during the months of this crisis. They went from being pastors to becoming public health experts, activity directors, technology specialists, and innovative church visionaries. They found ways to produce worship online and trained elderly parishioners to use Zoom. They set up phone trees and sent visitors to stand on the lawns of those who were ill. They organized meals for the community and fed hundreds of strangers. When church funds ran out, they wrote grant proposals. When volunteers failed to show, they filled the gaps, themselves. When spirits flagged, they became cheerleaders. When congregational anxiety crested, some bore the burden of their congregation's angst and even endured months of being the target of intense criticism.

CHURCH TRADITION

Susan remembers the assassination of President Kennedy for several reasons. Her elementary school was canceled. Her entire family spent several days that week huddled in front of the television listening to Walter Cronkite's reporting and absorbing the details of what had happened. The neighborhood streets were quiet as every family tried to learn the latest news and share the grief of the nation's leaders and first family. But something else happened that Susan remembers. She watched her father prepare his sermon for the Sunday following the assassination. She also remembers that when her father stepped into the pulpit in November 1963, the church was as full as it had ever been, and people grew especially quiet as he began to talk about how to live with hope even in the midst of a national crisis.

As a pastor herself in 2001, Susan thought of her father's experience in 1963 when she prepared her sermon for the weekend after September 11. She chose her words carefully because she anticipated a crowd unlike others, filled with people who were confused, scared about the future, and searching for the wisdom of faith. To be sure, her congregation grew still as she stepped into the pulpit that day too.

One of the prime roles of faith communities is to be places of meaning and strength when people face a crisis. Clergy always have big shoes to fill when they consider that the people they serve depend on them to offer the wisdom of their faith tradition in a crisis.

At the time of the collapse of the Twin Towers in New York City on September 11, 2001, a reporter interviewed a witness who had been walking on the sidewalk a mile north of the collapsing buildings. He was caked in dust as he described running back uptown as he watched in horror as the huge buildings were caving in and melting into the street. When he finally stopped and ducked into a safe alcove of a secure building, he reports that he looked back and began to pray. He could not remember the exact words he said, but he did remember reaching out to God.

Times of crisis shake the foundations of people's faith and shear them from their moorings. For generations it has been a time-honored response to seek the wisdom of a faith leader in periods of societal upheaval. Our nation is not alone in this tendency. In every society and culture people search for hope and comfort when life becomes uncertain. Being there in those very moments is one of the most vital and significant roles for faith leaders. Especially when people are fearful or their lives are in danger they come, weary but eager to find a perspective you can only find through faith. However, when this pandemic hit people could not access their spiritual leaders easily, and the clergy felt isolated from their flocks. No one knew how to change this situation. It would have been hard enough if all faith leaders could gather folks and talk to them in person about this international health crisis. It would have been overwhelming, but they already knew how to rise to the occasion in history's hard hinge moments. What made this pandemic so confounding was that clergy could not do what they knew how to do because they were forbidden to use many of their skills and gifts in the traditional ways.

Thrust into a time of worldwide uncertainty, widespread danger, and death, clergy felt stymied about how to make a difference and their sense of frustration is hard to overstate. They were forced to reimagine their trade and to reconsider the whole faith experience. They had to learn to pivot, but pivoting is more like side-stepping an obstacle on the sidewalk or taking a new turn on the dance floor. Faith leaders were not only pivoting; they had to learn to walk again and then embark on a journey through new territory, all without a map or GPS. Then they had to change their route repeatedly and experiment with new ways of doing religion, all while carrying these hulking churches and synagogues on their backs, old institutions long revered for their staying power and innate suspicion of change. They had to chart a new path by finding new ways to express faith and serve others while carrying everyone else along.

What made the clergy's response so extraordinary is the fact that religious institutions do not change easily. It's a big part of why people value them. In our rapidly changing world, churches are an anomaly. Maintaining tradition is a large part of their identity and what draws people to them. Change, while not unknown in religion, is rare. People don't go to church to be surprised. They go to practice time-honored rituals in ways that make folks feel connected to prior generations of believers. After all, isn't the divine unchanging and eternal? When innovation is needed in a faith community, it is proposed slowly, discussed thoroughly, then monitored carefully. Nothing in churches is precipitous, even when it might be advantageous. Often, people who serve as religious leaders have grown accustomed to this measured pace of change. Many clergy are attracted to this profession because they are comfortable in traditional institutions. They appreciate that leading a congregation can be a lot like steering an ocean liner, where course changes happen incrementally. Yet this pandemic required many clergy to become more nimble, as they navigated huge changes in rapid succession.

UNCONSCIOUS REVERSAL

Another factor that made this pandemic so challenging for clergy was that suddenly they were asked to become amateur epidemiologists. Accustomed to mingling in crowds, holding children, hugging the bereaved, or breaking bread for others, clergy now had to understand and consider the germ factor. The lives of the people they were leading depended on it.

Rev. Elizabeth Goodman of Lenox, Massachusetts, pointed out that this way of thinking about faith communities was a total reversal from the way that most clergy had been trained to think. Recalling the Gospels, she said Jesus described the kingdom of God in the New Testament like something that is contagious. He compared it to yeast spreading in flour, or mustard seeds growing out of bounds, or a miracle of feeding crowds of people. "God's message was supposed to spread like a contagion that no one could control. Implicit in Jesus' message is the idea that we don't ever have to worry about the contagion of the Good News of God. Having steeped herself in this interpretation," Goodman said that "it was almost more than she could adjust to, to start thinking like an epidemiologist, someone who is afraid of contagion." It seemed to go against her instincts as a Bible scholar. Prior to 2020 most clergy never weighed the costs of being open and vulnerable with strangers. They trusted that part of their job was to spread *good contagion*. Now, Goodman and all other clergy were forced to make a fundamental internal shift.

ISOLATION

Many clergy said they felt especially alone during the pandemic. While it was common for people in other professions to work from home, clergy felt responsible to be the guardians of sacred spaces. Many spent time in the church buildings alone, whether writing a sermon, overseeing the property or gaining technological skills needed to produce online worship programs.

Many clergy also told us they were extroverts. Their ability to mingle easily with groups of people and garner ideas from conversations had always been an asset before the pandemic. Extroverts find their best ideas in conversation, and get energy from crowds. People skills made clergy effective but also met a personal need. To lose the company of others was to lose stimulation and companionship. This new level of isolation brought a profound grief as they lost so many aspects of church life that nurtured their personalities and fed their souls. Without the people in the pews, one minister said, worship felt like a funeral. Others complained about how hollow it was to work in empty sanctuaries. Rev. Brad Bergquist, of Arvada, Colorado, summed up these feelings when he said, "I was not trained to do ministry other than in person; my skill is as a connector."

FUNDAMENTAL QUESTIONS

When pandemics hit like unexpected storms, people wonder why. In many parts of the Bible natural disasters are interpreted as signs of God's displeasure. In Genesis, when God decided the wickedness of humankind was irredeemable, God sent the flood. In Exodus, when God wanted to get Pharaoh's attention God sent ten plagues. These ancient stories rear their heads in our collective unconscious when crises occur suddenly without explanation. While we don't necessarily adopt that stance, we did wonder whether it simmered in the back of many minds as people everywhere questioned what caused this pandemic. Was there a fundamental lesson in it that we were supposed to learn?

Throughout history people of faith had also interpreted pandemics as a call to prayer. For many, a crisis of this proportion was meant to call us to fall to our knees. While such questions rarely were posed in the mainstream press, COVID-19 raised plenty of cosmic questions in people's minds. Though clergy reported that personally they responded to the crisis by deepening their devotion and increasing their prayer life, we also wondered if concerns about the possible origin or cause of the pandemic as a message from God added another unconscious burden for some. After all, it often falls to clergy to explain the unexplainable. Throughout history, if God was thought to be unhappy, it would fall to religious leaders to figure out why. In our survey we only found one pastor who interpreted the pandemic in biblical ways, as a call to repent. We want to be clear that we are not advocating for this interpretation of the pandemic or its cause, but we are aware that many people in various congregations were terrified in new ways and expected their religious leaders to be able to answer their questions about why this was happening, how long it would last, or even how to make it stop. As irrational as that may sound, to some, it may also have been part of the weight that faith leaders carried.

The changes in their work and the 24/7 solitude caused many religious leaders to ask basic questions about how to continue being a minister. In the Barna Research cited by many of the pastors we spoke to, and cited here earlier, many clergy changed jobs, retired early, or left the profession. In our small sample of active clergy, 28 percent of the people we talked to changed jobs in this pandemic. Of those, six retired, two resigned without another church to go to, five moved to new congregations, and four were intentional interim pastors between 2020 and 2022. It is possible that these transitions made it easier to continue the work as the grace of newness with its sense of exhilaration outweighed their anxiety. After our interviews we believe that anxiety weighed heavily in all their professional considerations.

The sense of frustration that most religious leaders felt is hard to overstate. Even though most clergy were overwhelmed, isolated, and out of their depth, they pressed on. Rev. Hollie Woodruff of Richmond, Virginia, explained, "Everyone was in a crisis, but clergy had to relearn their jobs." They stepped up because they felt responsible for their congregants and felt deep empathy and compassion for the people relying on them. Wherever they were when the pandemic hit—maternity leave, vacation, study abroad, or just feeling blind-sided in the midst of a busy spring—their initial drive was to get to their family of faith, to reach out to their people, and then shift into high gear to try to address the church's needs. These dedicated people, who were not accustomed to change, started down a path of continuous change week after week. As they steered their ships of faith, these ocean liners, not used to making quick turns or sudden course corrections, they headed into treacherous rapids.

In her historical novel about the bubonic plague, *Year of Wonders*, Geraldine Brooks told the story of an English village in 1666, another time of contagion four centuries ago.[2] When the plague hit, the people turned to their local minister to lead, to comfort and console but also to help them to find ways to stop the contagion. At the center of this novel is a clergyman who kept constant through it all, bearing his own losses bravely and simultaneously thinking of everyone. Though set in an era long before modern medicine, where plagues brought enormous loss of life, he shared

2. Brooks, *Year of Wonders*.

his gentle wisdom, put his own back into the work, and lived with hope. Through his tone and example, whether he was digging graves by hand or preaching at an outdoor worship service, he was a steady force for good in the community.

Like that fictional character, the clergy we spoke to were challenged to their core but also thrust into the center of a crisis where their leadership would make a difference to the people they knew and many they could never see or know. In so many communities, people credited their clergy for "getting them through this pandemic" with their steady, resourceful presence. Much has been written about the challenges for healthcare workers and teachers in this coronavirus pandemic, but the clergy in our churches faced challenges and made adjustments that were every bit as astonishing as their efforts were nothing short of herculean.

2

The Flywheel of Worship and How it Changed

"Despite the ongoing challenges of the pandemic, our faith community continued to thrive and grow and change. We lived into the promise that God is doing a new thing. Our strength and hope came—and continue to come—from the centrality of worship. No matter the circumstances, we met for worship: outside, inside, online, a bit of both. No matter what, we didn't stop worshiping our faithful God of love and grace."

—REV. NELL FIELDS, FALMOUTH, MASSACHUSETTS

REV. DEB GROHMAN IS an accomplished musician as well as a pastor in a Presbyterian church near Rochester, New York. On Saturday, March 14, 2020, the music school where she teaches canceled all her classes and encouraged her to set up her clarinet lessons online. The next day, Grohman led worship as usual. Following the service, she went out to lunch with her mom and son, Andrew (19), who had been sent home from Oberlin College in Ohio. While they were

The Perpetual Pivot

eating, the governor of New York closed all restaurants in the state, as the COVID-19 pandemic became an emergency. That afternoon Grohman learned how to use Zoom, in preparation for music lessons as well as for worship the following weekend.

With experience using Facebook Live, she enlisted her family to help her church pivot to online worship. Her husband, Willie, served as an organist in another church, and her son had skills as a computer technician. Together, they transformed their house into a worship service production studio. They called the internet company to boost their service and increase their ability to run all the equipment needed to produce good worship. Then, they reorganized their whole house. Grohman put her laptop on a music stand as she transformed her attic into a television studio. Meanwhile, on the ground floor, her husband lugged in audio equipment and recorded hymns on the family's grand piano for his own church and for Grohman's. On the second floor, Andrew turned his bedroom into a production studio, creating and showing PowerPoint slides for Grohman's services on his computer and inserting recorded music from his father on the first floor. Andrew also looked for images on the internet to create slides to illustrate his mom's sermon. But even with all this effort and coordination, they never missed a Sunday, as Grohman and her family worked as a creative team, making sure the cameras and lights worked, and then troubleshooting all the inevitable technical issues. Using their entire home for the next six months, they worked together to broadcast inspiring messages to their communities of faith from their home.

Grohman was not unusual in reporting that her stress was high and her hours long that spring. Though she was the only one we met who reconfigured her entire house to transform it into a broadcast studio, many clergy went to extraordinary lengths to lead worship services in 2020. Why did they do it? Why did clergy go to such effort to provide a worship experience during the pandemic when traditional worship was impossible? With a uniform sense of urgency, pastors across the nation all independently recognized it was imperative to figure out safe ways to worship. Why did worship matter so much? It mattered because most clergy see

The Flywheel of Worship and How it Changed

one of their primary roles to be leading their flocks in the worship of God. Clergy believe deeply in the practice of worship. They take pride in their services and the impact that they can make by reciting meaningful liturgy or offering inspiring sermons. Many faith leaders also find inspiration themselves in these very rituals.

For centuries it has been the ritual actions in faith communities that have brought meaning to life, setting the stage for prayers of petition, litanies of thanksgiving, space to listen to Scripture and reflect on its wisdom, time to sing praises to God. It has been the practice of worship over many generations that has held communities together in times of adversity and bonded families through times of travail. The regular spiritual discipline of gathering for worship services has provided a door to the transcendent realm that people of faith have come to rely on. It is in worship that many clergy have heard the call to serve in their profession, and the practice of leading worship has sustained many a faith leader throughout their own lives.

Clergy consider worship a central focus of their work. They prioritize a significant amount of time each week to prepare their weekly message. They lead their congregation, designing the flow of the service and crafting its emphasis. As the clear authorities on worship, it is one of the few areas where their ecclesiastical knowledge and judgment is undisputed. At the center of their calling to this profession is a commitment to share their insights on biblical wisdom, to frame life's rites of passage with sacred importance, and to help people find meaning in life. For many people, these worship services form the basis of religious expression. Rev. Jim Keck from Lincoln, NE described worship as the "flywheel" of faith. Worship collects the frustration and the hopes of the gathered people, brings them into a common orbit and disperses the congregation, renewed to serve God and one another in a wider orbit. Through weekly inspiration and community renewal in worship, people are spiritually fed and invigorated to do God's work. Good worship calms fear and renews people's optimism about life.

But these gatherings have always been held inside a sacred space, a sanctuary, with rituals that were efficacious in large part because they brought people together to experience a physical connection with each other and a symbolic connection to a transcendent power. In worship, people crowd into pews and sing with an abandon fueled by familiarity. Christians often share a common cup and pass bread from hand to hand when they celebrate the sacrament of communion. In worship, congregants hug strangers, hold hands, and kneel or stand shoulder to shoulder. In fact, it is in the experience of close human contact that worshipers encounter the sacred. Yet, in this crisis, the pandemic suddenly rendered all these expressions of faith off-limits. Initially, faith leaders were stymied and uncertain about how to perform their duties at all. Yet it was their commitment to the importance of these sacred communal gatherings, and their conviction that worship was more vitally important in a pandemic than ever, that compelled them to persevere. So they embarked on a journey for which no seminary course had prepared them and reinvented what they had been trained to do. They evaluated the essence of their work as worship leaders and refashioned their roles as preachers and presiders at the tables of faith.

Frontline workers in every way, these clergy continued to reach the lonely, comfort the grieving, pray for the sick, and hold their flocks together in worship. They also discovered how much they needed these worship services themselves. The stress of their jobs brought them to their knees. Many of them added extra prayer services, meant for others, only to discover these experiences helped them to brave on. They preached to cameras, in hollow sanctuaries, in recorded services that seemed only a pale approximation of what clergy loved about worship. Yet, to their surprise, there was often power and efficacy to the words they spoke, because they spoke them with real conviction in a time of crisis. Staring into the eye of a camera, many discovered they were not only reaching people near and far who searched for meaning and a sacred bond online; they were also speaking to their own weary hearts.

Religious leadership is often divided into three categories—Priest, Pastor, and Prophet. In the priestly role, clergy regard creating and giving a service as a non-negotiable assignment, with a deadline every seven days. The pandemic did not change that. When congregations could not gather in person, clergy realized they needed to quickly master the technology needed to produce worship online. One pastor reported that when the decision was made to close the church doors, she had just two days to plan and produce a worship experience for her people online, a hefty assignment that required all her creativity, flexibility, and abundant grace under pressure.

Yes, clergy demonstrated their strong work ethic during the pandemic, but it was much more than that. They all believed that the worship of God was not optional, especially during the pandemic. They believed in the efficacy of practicing their faith in good times and valued it even more in a crisis. Many told us, with pride, that they had not missed a Sunday from the time the pandemic started. It was not just the comfort they hoped to convey through their sermons, it was a conviction that people in a crisis needed spiritual resources. People living with anxiety and enduring great loss needed faith. Many recalled the initial days of the pandemic in striking detail, especially as it began to dawn on them that all the rituals they knew by heart and had recited for years were being suspended indefinitely or needed a complete revision to meet the public health standards. It is hard to overstate the impact of these health-related restrictions on worship services.

Additionally, for some the idea of worshiping virtually went against their grain. They believed the personal experience of praying and praising God with others points symbolically to an intimacy with God. For them, the pandemic challenged their core beliefs about how to approach the divine. Many kept vigil in their sanctuaries, burning candles or reciting prayers alone as representatives of their people. Many refused to stay at home, and worked alone in their church buildings. One man made it his policy to preside at baptisms, weddings, and funerals in person throughout the pandemic, so strong was his belief in offering rites of passage in person in a timely manner. Admittedly, he risked his own health, but his decision points to a bedrock commitment to the vital importance

The Perpetual Pivot

of the incarnational aspect of worship. The importance of bodily presence cannot be overestimated in the Judeo-Christian tradition. The Old Testament is full of stories about Hebrew patriarchs and prophets like Abraham, Jacob, Moses, and Samuel, who had personal experiences of communicating with God or hearing God's voice in person. Christian faith is based on the belief that God became human, incarnate, in the body of Jesus of Nazareth. Across many faith traditions is the understanding that connecting to God is not a spiritual enterprise alone, but part of a bodily experience. Initially, the pandemic restrictions were jarring to clergy but also profoundly confusing.

At the start of the pandemic half of the people we interviewed streamed services on Facebook Live. Most led services from a home office, a dining table or even a bedroom. Before long, twenty eight percent of those we interviewed migrated to worshiping on Zoom because this platform allowed congregants to see one another. The Zoom platform soon occupied a central part of many congregation's tool kits for worship, study, fellowship and all gatherings. This platform became easy for people of every age to access. Plus churches could control who attended Zoom meetings or worship and put boundaries around this new sacred space. Zoom also allowed people to greet one another in breakout rooms online, a welcome feature in a time of isolation.

Without exception, clergy reported being impressed by the efforts of elderly congregants to learn how to use online platforms like Zoom. The very demographic clergy worried about most proved to be highly motivated to remain connected to church friends. Even when their internet connection was poor, senior citizens banded together to drive one another to someone's porch to pick up an internet connection in order to worship remotely. We lost track of how many stories we heard of parishioners in their eighties and nineties who managed to connect to a worship service through video or audio links.

As soon as it seemed safe to gather a skeletal crew to produce online worship from their sanctuaries, many clergy returned to that sacred space to lead worship. Formerly pristine chancel floors were now covered with wires as they transformed altar areas into recording studios complete with microphones, cameras, and special lighting. This allowed congregants to see much beloved church furnishings and appointments: pulpits, stained-glass windows, communion tables, baptismal fonts, banners, and all the other favorite features of their spiritual homes. Some parishioners were moved to tears at the first sight in weeks of their sanctuary's interior.

TECHNOLOGY CHALLENGES

Technology was a huge hurdle for all the church leaders we surveyed. Some newer and larger congregations had tech teams in place, but most did not. This technology transition posed a steep learning curve for most clergy. People drawn to the pastorate or rabbinate are more likely to study philosophy or English than computer engineering as they prepare for their careers. Most clergy told us that technology skills were not in their wheelhouse. Many did not know what equipment was even needed to produce worship online. Some pastors found they lacked a strong enough internet connection in their houses of worship, never mind microphones or cameras for filming and recording a service. This crisis required them to become experts in an area where they often felt inadequate.

"Tech was a headache," recalled one pastor. "We read everything we could find online, but still it wasn't enough." Rev. Leah Fowler, of Leoina, New Jersey, agreed. "Tech was the biggest challenge, even as a Gen X pastor; it was such hard work with so little support. My wife is a television producer in New York City, and she helped me put the services together for weeks. Still, we had to borrow equipment and we both felt the weight of it all on our shoulders." Another pastor told us she recruited her stepson, a recent graduate from film school in Manhattan. He assumed responsibility and then taught her everything he could so she could progress from using her cell phone in her office to using a movie-making program on her laptop. It took a while but with these new skills, worship became much less of a headache and more of a creative enterprise.

This one anecdote reveals what clergy so desperately needed. They needed to be matched up with mentors from the film industry who could give them a crash course in filming, editing, and production. Many we spoke to would have welcomed that option.

Larger congregations with livestreaming experience and communication experts on staff had a jump start when the pandemic set in. But even churches with cameras and sound boards in place recognized the need for upgrades. Fort Lauderdale pastor Rev. Patrick Wrisley leads a large congregation that prides itself on offering the best worship. Yet, he bought robotic cameras, feeling pressure to maintain a polished service for fear his people would wander to other online services that appeared more professional. Congregations of all sizes complained about the sound quality and the camera shots. Though clergy put a lot of time into learning to edit film and produce video, many pastors felt they were being evaluated by new standards. We heard this comment enough that we wondered why, suddenly, all this effort was not enough. We concluded that during the pandemic, people who spent much more time on screens now judged worship by different standards, expecting their local congregation to produce services that met the standards of television studio productions. It was not uncommon to spend untold hours producing a special piece of music with pictures inserted to illustrate the words, only to have a parishioner complain about the camera angle that was used.

Producing online worship required the continual ability to pivot. "There was no time to stop, no moments to celebrate," said one. As clergy shifted from Facebook to YouTube, they were constantly adjusting. "It wasn't just that we were building the airplane while we flew, we were also flying blind," said Rev. Wrisley

STEEP LEARNING CURVE

Preaching has long been regarded as the quintessential art of ministry, and sermons can seal a pastor's reputation. The pandemic forced clergy to learn a new way to preach, and for many this was one of the hardest challenges. People who had honed their skills

The Flywheel of Worship and How it Changed

speaking to a congregation in person, had grown to depend on the energy of a live audience. They relied on glances of recognition, smiles of encouragement, or even questions in a listener's eyes. All these visual cues provided feedback to help preachers gauge whether people were engaged, confused, bored, or lost. Starved for that immediate feedback, many pastors found it impossibly hard to make the transition to a camera. They told us that they had to learn a whole new way to preach because nothing felt right. We also heard from some people who adjusted to preaching online. They said, in time, they grew to enjoy looking into a camera while they imagined their audience.

Nearly everyone said learning to create online worship was one of the most stressful challenges of their careers as church leaders. In the beginning, each service proved to be an exhausting exercise with last minute changes, technical corrections, and complex adjustments based on changing public health requirements. The congregations that were fortunate were those few that had the good fortune to have a clergy person who had experience or aptitude in using online platforms. In Brookline, Massachusetts, Rev. John Sweet began an interim in a church where he was needed as much for his technological prowess as his skills as a pastor and preacher. When the pandemic started he was in such demand as someone who could create worship easily that he produced services from home that were broadcast at two churches, one in Boston and the other in Providence, Rhode Island. He quickly developed a popular set of classes for children and youth as well as study groups for adults.

As soon as the pandemic started, Rev. Emily Keller from Dartmouth, Massachusetts, set out to learn how to record worship, edit film, upload her services to the internet, and post them—all herself. It was labor intensive and proved to be very time-consuming. The quote for installing the right equipment in her sanctuary was over $25,000. But Keller's adult son researched the problem and installed the equipment himself for one tenth the original cost. Finally, when the technology proved too expensive in terms of her own time, Keller found volunteers, but it required three volunteers to accomplish what *she had been doing every week, for a year, which was eye-opening for everyone.*

Though most clergy we interviewed began livestreaming a worship service taped in an empty sanctuary, eventually 20 percent of clergy we interviewed began producing pre-recorded worship. That meant they recorded the sermons and prayers mid-week so they could be edited, often by the clergy themselves, and then combined with pre-recorded music or photography. Then they created a final production they would upload to a website or YouTube channel for the weekend.

As they matured as online worship leaders, they asked harder questions about how to produce appealing services. Rev. Hollie Woodruff of Richmond, Virginia, discovered the book *Think Like a Filmmaker*,[1] and it influenced her to reinterpret a lot of things she had taken for granted in worship. She decided to shorten her hour-long service to half the time. Research from Facebook confirmed that twenty-four minutes or less was optimal for online worship services, because people who tuned into online worship had a much shorter attention span than folks in the pews for an in-person service. Clergy accustomed to planning one-hour services had to reimagine worship that was less than half as long—a major adjustment. In scaling down her service, Woodruff evaluated the theological importance of every element, then stripped worship of all but these essential elements. She eliminated litanies, extra readings, children's sermons, and liturgical chants and hymns to craft a leaner experience, ideal for an online audience. Many clergy abandoned their old checklist of prescribed readings or sung responses because this format that had been second nature for in-person worship no longer made sense. Ironically, these new online services began to appeal to new people who had never attended worship before but were seeking spiritual or religious inspiration online. But the changes were a hard sell for some life-long members, seasoned worshipers who did not appreciate the quicker tempo and complained about the loss of familiar church practices.

---

1. McFee, *Think Like a Filmmaker*.

The Flywheel of Worship and How it Changed Budget!!! (or "Tech doesn't grow on trees")

Most faith communities do not have much of a budget, if any, for worship, and all the clergy we spoke to had concerns about how to pay for new expenditures needed to produce worship online. They underwrote the bulk of the cost of a worship service through the salaries of clergy, musicians, and other staff. While central to the life of a congregation, worship was never a high ticket item because it relied on the creativity of the religious leader who typically recited the liturgy and gave a sermon. Once a congregation invested in a building, furniture, and hymnals, they were mostly finished, other than utilities and perhaps the occasional bill for candles. Most congregations could not even imagine all the financial needs for cameras, lighting, teleprompters, online music, or technical training for the clergy.

Many ministers described their own internal calculus about how to revamp worship without a budget. While equipment like microphones, sound boards, cameras, tripods, even computers would not break the bank in most church budgets, it was striking how frugal the clergy were. They took their fiduciary responsibility so seriously that they recruited volunteers, found free technology advice and training, and pressed family members into service. They worked hard to save money, but it took a toll on them to operate with this level of economy. One minister lost track of how many times she had to retape her Easter service because of the shaky internet in her building and her church's reluctance to upgrade it. No one we encountered seemed to be taking advantage of this crisis. There was no hint of anyone manipulating the congregation to buy new equipment that wasn't essential. In fact, many clergy tightened their own belts and subsidized the church by borrowing equipment, contributing from their own personal equipment or by going without. But there were costs to this level of thrift, too. It took longer to develop online worship, so the worship suffered. One pastor told us it took five and a half hours to film a half hour service she could live with. Pastors ourselves, we wonder whether this toll, largely underestimated, can also be seen in the numbers of people who later questioned their calling.

Several ministers took a different approach.

In one congregation several people were taking a filmmaking course and really stepped up to help put the worship services online. Their pastor went to the sanctuary with a reader and musician for a filming session each week, and these novice filmmakers would film it. This proved to be so effective that later in 2020 the congregation hired an experienced filmmaker to record both the band and the choir. He created a music library for the pastor to use when she designed worship. Then she pivoted to ask the filmmaker to teach some youth in the church how to make videos that they could put online for the church.

❖

Just days into the pandemic, Rev. Eileen Morris of Slatersville, Rhode Island, called a local filmmaker who was working on a documentary for public television in Boston. She told him she needed him to come film her worship service. She found he was willing to help for free, at first. He met her at the church sanctuary and videotaped the services and initially donated his services for four weeks, which Morris assumed would be enough. But when the pandemic lasted longer, she persuaded the congregation to pay the filmmaker because he was a professional, and the professionalism showed. In the end, the church paid for sixty-four weeks of filmmaking.

What set Morris apart from other people we interviewed is how quickly she understood that she needed help. And, importantly, she was not afraid to ask her congregation for that support. Her decision meant the church had professional worship online from day one for an affordable price. All churches have tight budgets, but in supporting a filmmaker this church bought two things: great worship and time for their pastor to focus on pastoral care, administrative leadership, Bible study, and other things she was more uniquely qualified to do.[2]

2. Morris arranged with a local filmmaker from an indie studio south of Boston to do four worship services. He volunteered for those, and then the

The Flywheel of Worship and How it Changed

Several pastors explored other approaches to raising money for new technology. Some developed a budget for upgrades and announced a fundraising challenge. It was a logical pitch that the online public could understand. "We want to bring you the best worship, and for that we need some new equipment. Here's how you can help." Churches who did this often raised more than they expected. Almost every clergyperson we spoke to eventually decided to upgrade their internet and purchase new equipment during the pandemic. Rev. Fritz Fowler of Lansdale, Pennsylvania, predicts that a tech budget will need to be a fundamental portion of every church budget going forward in the same way that a budget for music is standard. A few people found training for pastors to make this pivot to online worship but resources were few and far between.

WORSHIP OUTSIDE

High-tech online services weren't the only worship innovation. From Atlanta to Anchorage outdoor worship was a welcome alternative in the spring and summer of 2020. Clergy felt liberated as they set up services on beaches, in gardens and woods, at labyrinths and fire pits. Congregations gathered on mountain trails and desert paths, on patios beside the church building or on grassy slopes. Rev. Kathleen Clark led her people out on the grass in East Arlington, Vermont, where they gazed at a Norman Rockwell-like scene of cattle and verdant farmland during worship. Their service under a tent became so popular that parishioners now intend to worship outdoors every summer.

However, the physical and technical work of leading worship outside was not to be underestimated, and again, it often fell to the clergy. Rev. Rebecca McElfrish had the ideal location for outside worship at her church in Sahuarita, Arizona, but she reported that she had to arrive three hours early to transport chairs, tables,

---

church paid him for sixty-four weeks of worship, enough work to support this filmmaker part-time during the pandemic, but the church negotiated a price for this that they could afford.

microphones, cables, keyboards, and speakers outside before they were ready to welcome the congregation. Often the sounds of traffic or the threat of rain added some suspense, but congregations were grateful to be together safely in community. Many such services filled a need and thrived.

A number of clergy ran worship services in their parking lots with the audio broadcast through a radio link people could access on the car radio. This was a very successful model that included worship and often a drive-through communion so people could receive the sacrament safely from their vehicles while the clergy stood in their robes handing out bread and cups of wine. This model proved successful for many months as clergy preached in parking lots, and conducted rites of passage in inventive ways. They baptized children through car windows. Rev. Mary Bauer, from Appleton, Wisconsin, organized their rite of confirmation as a drive-through experience. Families drove up to a flatbed trailer, where the clergy were stationed. The confirmand and parents would get out and climb onto the trailer one family at a time for the ceremony of blessing. Others devised ways to lead prayer meetings, and even memorial services out of doors in 2020–21.

While some clergy went outside to meet their people others used visual resources to illustrate their message by bringing the outside in.

Rev. Mary Bauer went to work mastering PowerPoint and learning to make videos on Filmora. Then she incorporated these tools to help her people visualize her message when she preached. In a sermon on the wilderness, Bauer included footage of walking in the woods. When she preached about evil spreading, she baked bread and demonstrated her message through her baking.

❧

Rev. Candi Ashenden, of Athol, Massachusetts, also learned to edit film, in spring 2020, as a way to enhance her online worship services. At first she photographed natural scenes and took video images in natural settings to use as backdrops for the prayer and hymn portions of her services. Then, that spring she had to pick up a teenager at school in Colorado and attend a college graduation for her son in California. Contemplating the trips, she was inspired to take photographs and video footage at nationally known sacred spots along her routes.

She organized an itinerary to include the Grotto of Redemption in Indiana, a basilica in St. Louis, the Baynton Canyon Vortex and the Chapel of the Holy Cross (both in Sedona, Arizona) Death Valley, and the Redwoods National Park. She integrated footage from these places into her services and the new images of natural beauty added variety and zest to services planned for her parishioners who'd been confined to their homes for weeks. Through her photography, she took her people on the journey with her, and shared experiences that they couldn't have themselves. This completely changed the way she imagined worship, and everything became much more visual for her as a worship leader.

Ashenden's creative eye and ingenuity about how to use her own family trips transformed how she shared her faith by illustrating it in new ways at every service. Clergy who found ways to "think like a filmmaker" used the pandemic to find ways to enhance worship by exploring the use of visuals in online worship. They reevaluated everything they thought they knew about worship and changed the camera angle, added backdrops, considered lighting, ordered quilts and teleprompters. They used photographs during musical interludes and simulated stained glass windows, all to invite worshippers to find their spiritual home in this online space. Those who explored the creative potential of online worship found in it a new art form.

MUSIC

When the COVID pandemic began, the first widely publicized super spreader event was a choir rehearsal in Washington state where fifty-two singers got sick. As a result of this experience, choir directors were very nervous about leading chorus rehearsals or performances. They canceled all choir events and proceeded with caution for months. Because music is such a key feature of most worship experiences, eliminating choral music was unsatisfying, but adding it proved to be challenging. Most clergy sought safe work-arounds. They recorded organists playing a hymn or attempted to coordinate recordings of singers at home on Zoom. None of this was easy, but copyright laws posed an even bigger challenge.

Copyright laws forbid the online use of most recorded music, and even with an international health emergency, those copyright laws remained unbending. Facebook routinely disqualified or disrupted whole worship services mid-stream when they included copyrighted recorded music. All congregations needed additional permission to add recorded church music to online worship. It would not be an overstatement to say that clergy were consumed with copyright concerns in the early days of the pandemic. Finding music to complement their message or comfort their people was hard enough, but then began the daunting task of determining how to include it.

In a few congregations choral directors used special editing programs to blend the voices of individual singers. Each singer recorded themselves at home as a solo voice, sending it to the director to be combined with other voices to create the sound of a chorus. Listening later, church members reported weeping as they heard the familiar tunes they had missed to much. The experience was profound, but the process required many hours of editing.

Rev. Gordon Pullan, pastor in North Hadley, Massachusetts, and his organist Chris White, a music professor at the University of Massachusetts Amherst, teamed up to create a choir that was eventually featured on National Public Radio. Initially, Pullan felt caught flatfooted when the pandemic started. Soon, he developed a podcast with a sermon message and a virtual choir. Then he and White challenged the singers to record their own voices individually so they could combine the digital recordings to get the sound of a choir. The energy generated by this project exploded. People from the community, friends from childhood, and seasoned church singers all joined the online chorus. Pullan marveled at the time it took White to transform twenty individual digital recordings into

The Flywheel of Worship and How it Changed

one coherent stream of music, but the results were so impressive that the podcasts garnered lots of local attention and eventually national radio exposure.

But the project did something else for this congregation and for Pullan. It brought people together in a cooperative experience that was uplifting and hopeful.[3] This whole project evolved out of the creative partnership between this pastor and organist and sent a needed message that the church had not been defeated but was still the place in town to bring people together in innovative ways, even during a pandemic.

Like Ashenden, Pullan found ways to use the historical moment of crisis to let his own creativity unfold. In doing so he took worship to a new level, surprising himself and his people, and inspiring everyone with a sense of hope that even a pandemic could not stop. Somehow this spirit of innovation spread hope because it felt like a phoenix was emerging from the ashes of so much that felt like loss.

THE GIFTS OF THIS EXPERIENCE

Amid all the challenges, stress, and struggles of providing worship experiences to spiritually hungry congregations, many clergy also discovered unforeseen gifts. Forced to reimagine worship, some clergy used the crisis to question old habits that had grown familiar but now seemed unimportant or even outdated. No longer satisfied with familiar modes of worship, clergy reimagined service bulletins, offering plates, and how to take communion more meaningfully. Zoom allowed Rabbi Carl Perkins to preside over a funeral in Philadelphia, a wedding in Denver, and a bris in Boston. While he could reach a much wider audience now, he acknowledged that his new accessibility also changed those rituals and caused him to ponder how to make them meaningful.

This process of rethinking holy rituals and spaces came with trade-offs. Some clergy worried about the changes, but others

---

3. Kaufman, "For Some Church-Goers."

reported a newfound sense of adventure. The crisis eventually made them bolder. Adversity brought both stress and a curious kind of freedom. With fewer rules in place, some clergy actually felt exhilarated and enjoyed a season of fresh creativity.

Rev. Robyn Gray of Washington, Connecticut, reported that she grew less likely to ask permission from her members and just tried new things as inspiration moved her. She started offering daily devotionals that aired on social media, and they became her own spiritual discipline. Writing the daily devotionals improved her preaching, as she learned quickly how to find the meaningful nugget in any scripture lesson.

New podcasts and online devotions blossomed, many with audiences online that extended far beyond the parish boundaries. The intimacy of working together in these sacred spaces set the stage for deep bonds between the clergy and musicians or tech staff engaging in this creative process. When the team included family members of these clergy, the bonds became additionally close. Rev. Deb Grohman was not the only pastor who enlisted her spouse and son to produce worship. Several spoke movingly about the new intimacy they felt working with their families. Whether pressed into service to read scripture or to run a camera, people bonded as they faced technical setbacks or celebrated small victories. Church sanctuaries, now empty save for these creative teams, became holy ground in new ways.

Stunning examples of creativity blossomed in this pandemic. In North Hadley, Pullan reinvented his Maundy Thursday service, inviting hospital nurses to do the readings, which gave that liturgy a whole new layer of meaning. His podcast, using the handle "Prayers in a Time of Tweets, Pandemic, Racism, and Violence" reached a wider and wider audience. For Easter 2020, Rev. Pam Werntz found local artists in Boston who lent her life-sized puppets that she placed around the sanctuary as though they were seated in the pews. The puppets showed up as the camera panned the pews, delighting viewers with a "crowd" on that feast day in her Episcopal church. Across the nation, complete strangers gravitated to online worship services and grew loyal to the preachers, so loyal they sent letters of appreciation, some with checks inside.

CHRISTMAS LIKE NO OTHER

Christmas 2020 arrived more than nine months after the lockdown began, and clergy across the country reached deep into their wells of creativity to plan safe celebrations. As always, clergy believed their own people needed a message of hope only the churches could provide. They also recognized that this was a message the wider community was hungry for and this holiday was typically a time when people turned to faith communities annually for an inspiring message. Many clergy outdid themselves that year. They commissioned music, mailed creches, delivered Advent calendars, collected videos of people lighting their candles, organized ways to share holiday greetings and unleashed myriad playful ways to celebrate the occasion.

Given the COVID public health restrictions, they found ways to observe this winter holiday all out of doors. Rev. Stuart Spencer of Moorestown, New Jersey, set up a service around fire pits on the church patio on the night before Christmas Eve. On a chilly December evening his people gathered with blankets and sleeping bags, as a new tradition was born.

❋

Rev. David Shirey of Lexington, Kentucky, created a set of tableaus outside along the church's driveway that told the story of the birth of Jesus. His "Windows to Bethlehem" display depicted angels, shepherds, wise men, and the Holy Family on a route that cars could follow, while listening to the story on car radios tuned to the church's radio frequency. With the sacred music of the season in the background people could hear the narration of this central story of faith. The display delighted his people and attracted people from the wider community as they celebrated Christmas together safely.

❋

In a similar way Rev. Jim Keck of Lincoln, Nebraska, wanted to create a nativity experience that would draw the whole community to his church, where normally they see four-thousand worshippers at Christmas. His first plan was to create a walking tour through the decorated sanctuary, complete with all the usual poinsettias, candles and festive banners, but a new variant of the virus forced him to shelve that idea and pivot to another concept. Instead, he hired a lighting company and a puppet theater to create a festive outdoor experience similar to the one in Kentucky, where people heard the story of the birth of Jesus along the expansive drive around his church. The drive-through story of Christmas at his church was not inexpensive, but it was so unique that it attracted visitors from all over the state, and before long, television vans parked on the church lawn garnered publicity and media coverage that proved priceless.

Many clergy felt determined to create nativity experiences for the community, often navigating logistical obstacles but in the process they discovered that folks everywhere were tired, scared, and hungry for the hope and wonder at the heart of the Christmas message. Their efforts were met with gratitude and the wholehearted appreciation of parishioners as well as the wider public.

❄

In our own church Susan planned a Christmas Eve service around a live nativity concept on the lawn. We recruited church members to take the parts of shepherds and angels, along with Mary and Joseph. We asked a local woman studying opera to sing and a local farmer to bring a couple of sheep, which he did. Unfortunately, we did not realize the farmer would also bring some goats and a cow until he arrived with the entire menagerie. We put all the livestock into a small pen meant for a few sheep. The opera singer had not performed in months and decided not to wear a mask, which worried us. In the week before Christmas, cast members kept changing as the illness afflicted different families.

In the end, nothing really went as planned. Susan had to recruit the characters for the drama from people who arrived early for worship. The last-minute cast was honored and enthusiastic, however unrehearsed. This became apparent as we started reading the gospel lessons. To manage the chaos, Peggy quickly donned a costume and embedded herself into the tableaus, offering whispered directions dressed as a star. This worked, until the goats smelled food in a woman's purse. They easily jumped the fence, followed by the cow. Several ushers managed to restrain the animals and return them to the pen. The whole experience was so completely opposite to the well-rehearsed services we ordinarily had on this high holiday. Yet people on the lawn that night told us with tears that it was the best Christmas service they'd ever attended. So, we had to wonder about what makes a service meaningful. That night, it was clear that perfection is overrated.

※

From many states we heard similar stories about grateful strangers on the lawns of churches telling faith leaders these services made a difference to them as communities everywhere turned to the Church for inspiration in this crisis.

3

What about the People?

My superpower is my ability to talk to people face to face, to sit with someone and know what they are feeling. It's my ability to turn into another person. But it is a skill honed through in-person encounters. In the pandemic, I was being asked to put all that aside.
—Rev. Elizabeth Goodman, Lenox, Massachusetts

"I've never seen anything like this in thirty-five years of pastoral ministry."
—Rev. Brad Bergquist, Arvada, Colorado

In one United Methodist church in Des Moines, Washington, Rev. Joanne Brown shepherded a busy congregation in the Pacific Northwest, where the majority of her church leaders lived in a Methodist-run retirement village not far from the church. The arrangement allowed for an easy flow between a large pool of active volunteers, many life-long Methodists, and frequent opportunities for pastoral visits so Brown was in constant contact with people in the retirement village. However, at the onset of COVID-19, this continuing care community instituted strict restrictions. Suddenly no one in the retirement community was allowed to leave the campus and non-residents were forbidden to come onto the campus. That included their local Methodist pastor Rev. Brown.

While her congregants understood the restrictions, they experienced them as an utter lockdown. The lay leaders were confined to their buildings and sometimes their rooms for many weeks and even months at a time, unable to attend worship services or receive visits. The new safety measures put Brown in an untenable position: "I could no longer do my job."

The Methodist Church guidelines for church building use, like those of most Protestant denominations at the time, also forbade people from congregating in the church building. Brown felt torn between her commitment to her bishop and her own call to serve her people, torn between the official guidelines and her pastoral responsibility to be the face of hope and comfort for her flock. Loyalty to both her people and her church was wrenching and brought on a spiritual and professional frustration that tore her apart. When people approached her with requests that tugged at her heartstrings, she could not turn her back on them, so she labored to find safe ways to allow people to be together. For example, a member of many decades died of cancer during the pandemic, and the family asked Brown to officiate at a service for her. Knowing such a service would not be possible in the sanctuary, Brown agreed to attend the memorial service in a private home, although she knew it was in violation of her denomination's guidelines. Another member had stage-four cancer but her children wanted to celebrate one final birthday with her. They asked Brown if she could find a way for them to use the church hall, which had been off-limits for weeks. Brown allowed them access, before the building was officially open, scrupulously making sure things were clean and carefully handing off the keys to the building. At the time, fears of spreading the virus made people especially cautious about passing things from one person to another. In the end, the decision to allow the birthday party resulted in a completely safe celebration that brought comfort to this family two weeks before their mother died.

The Perpetual Pivot

❦

The second vital portion of a faith leader's responsibility is being a pastor. The word "pastor" comes from the Latin root that means shepherd, "to lead to pasture, set to grazing, cause to eat." The title "pastor" is an honorific used by many clergy because more than any other word, "pastor" defines their role, especially in Protestant congregations. Being a good shepherd is essential to successful congregational leadership and a central part of the work. Clergy feel responsible to care for members of their congregations, in all seasons of life. The pressure they felt to respond to the needs of their people in this pandemic cannot be overstated.

Pastors are often among the first people who are notified when a baby is born. They are the ones summoned when a person is about to die. They sit with a family that faces a difficult diagnosis or waits for test results. It is clergy who are called when couples seek advice in a failing relationship or a family quarrel. It's clergy who hear about the anniversary of a death or a grief that won't let go. Clergy listen as people confess their gravest doubts or most embarrassing transgressions. They are the ones people turn to when they don't know where else to go. Clergy hold many secrets safe. They listen when people ponder life's hardest questions. They go where they are needed: to backyards and hospital rooms, to nursing homes and hospice centers. Good religious leaders develop the ability to stand with people when no one has adequate answers. They do this with their physical presence.

It is only in person that you can "read the room," see the gestures, feel the depth of passion or silence. It is only when you are there in person that you pick up on the chemistry between family members or sense the loneliness in a marriage, even when there are no outward signs of it. It's only in person that clergy develop the intuition to recognize when someone's fear is louder than the optimism in their words. There is no substitute for the comfort a pastor can bring by physically being there, in person.

The COVID pandemic undermined all these efforts to minister and presented a huge dilemma for faith leaders. Banned from hospitals, nursing homes, and private homes, they were stripped of their ability to use their superpowers. They were unable to offer their wisdom or comfort in person, and many felt especially helpless.

In these ways, it was the perfect storm. Initially the elderly seemed most vulnerable, and public health officials along with hospital and nursing home administrators curtailed pastoral visitation. However, those vulnerable people were then consigned to isolation, many condemned to die alone with no spiritual succor. As thousands of people in many congregations were dying or left alone terrified in their rooms, clergy were sidelined. Some facilities allowed the dispensation for last rites or prayers at the time of death, but even that was rare for many months.

Clergy everywhere had to navigate an obstacle course of public health restrictions, denominational guidelines, and people's personal needs. In all our dozens of interviews, we heard not one single story about a pastor being reckless or cavalier. Instead, clergy spoke of a weighty responsibility to serve others, caring for them emotionally and spiritually. Father Greg Christakos of Marlborough, Massachusetts, spoke for many when he said the hardest part of the pandemic for him was the inability to be with people in life's precious moments, whether it was the birth of a baby or loss of someone dear. "These visits at a window were not the same!" he said. Many clergy described their frustration and worry about widows or widowers who lived alone, the elderly who seemed somewhat confused at the best of times, the forgetful who were struggling on a good day, the "lost lambs" in every congregation. The concern we heard most was that it was almost impossible to stay in touch and to "keep people together."

When they did visit with a parishioner with COVID, pastors often played a pivotal role, and these encounters were poignant for them and for their people.

❧

Rev. Quentin Chin of Southampton, Massachusetts, visited patients in the COVID wards. He said, "Dressed in personal protective equipment, I gained entry by unzipping a vinyl curtain which kept extraneous personnel out of the ward. It translated to no visible signs of life in the ward, other than people lying in their beds. The wards were deathly quiet. At that time most nursing homes did not permit families to visit until the patient's life was almost at an end. Thus, COVID patients were starved for any human contact. Yet some of the nursing homes had tablets which I could borrow to bring to a patient so that they could 'visit' with a family member on the outside. I became a bystander for these visits which were often heartbreaking as the 'visitor' was simultaneously visibly moved and frustrated to see their loved one without being able to hug them or share intimacies in the presence of a bystander they did not know. When a tablet was not available I would call the family member to report on a visit. Then, I could hear the weary frustration in their voice. They savored every word, and even though the initial encounter with the patient might not have been more than five or six minutes, our conversations released their anxieties and gave them a moment's comfort and assurance in the long trajectory of their loved one's illness . . . I often left these visits drained."

❋

So much of what makes pastors effective is the personal touch, the empathic presence. It is the ability to be a gifted listener or an intuitive counselor. It is the ability seasoned pastors have of knowing when to say something important and when to trust the healing power in a shared silence. When pastors become trusted guides and advisors for their people, it is because they can sense who needs their advice and who needs an extra prayer. In ordinary times many pastors might scan a crowd, perhaps from the pulpit or walking down a church hallway. In a few moments, they can "take the pulse" of their people. They notice who is talking to whom and who feels left out, who is angry, or who needs a hug. In short order, pastors can work a room, gauging the energy and deciding where to put their efforts. During the pandemic, they felt they were in the dark. Unable to gather people in person, they felt helpless to make these professional evaluations. Who was struggling? Who was lonely? Who seemed depressed?

GETTING CREATIVE

Remarkably, the crisis unleashed some creative and life-changing ways to minister. Some doubled down on communications. They developed labor intensive programs to reach their people at home. They wrote devotional booklets and mailed them. They recorded CDs of services for folks without computers and devised ways to deliver care packages to many a porch. In Dartmouth, Massachusetts, Rev. Emily Keller reported making hundreds of phone calls along with sending dozens of cards and personal notes to her people. But no matter how much effort clergy exerted, some parishioners continued to feel lonely. Some were angry about being so isolated; some blamed the church for failing to do more. Clergy speculated that some anger was linked to widespread anxiety, but still that was hard to alleviate and harder to absorb without feeling defensive.

Some ministers also cited an unexpected resilience among senior citizens who reminded them that they had endured many crises in the decades of their long lives—wars, polio epidemic, AIDS—and they believed that they could ride this out, too. Still others were grateful beyond all measure at their pastor's commitment to finding people on the margins or people they had not heard from. In this national emergency with its widespread isolation, the call from a pastor or rabbi became a lifeline. For many seeing their pastor's zeal for keeping the flock together increased their devotion

❖

In Susan's church early in the pandemic when one man died of COVID we decided to hold a hymn sing on his lawn since his funeral was being postponed. Neighbors and parishioners arrived as the choir sang. This event touched so many people that church members

started a group to sing for those who were elderly, ill, or isolated. Standing outside the window of a woman on hospice care her church family joined in chorus with her children circling her bedside. There were few dry eyes as the familiar melodies of faith filled the air. For these singers, this program also ministered to them offering them all a sense of purpose during the pandemic.

❖

At the height of the pandemic Rev. Laura Folkwein of Bozeman, Montana, initiated nightly prayers on Zoom. Inviting her people to share evening prayers together in unison reminded them that though they were separate in body they remained one in spirit, through the power of prayer. The words she chose were traditional ones from The Book of Common Prayer *and served as a time-honored reminder that faith can be a strong aid, especially in adversity. "Keep watch, dear Lord, with those who work or watch or weep this night," the evening prayer says, "and give your angels charge over those who sleep. Tend the sick, Lord Christ; Give rest to the weary; bless the dying, sooth the suffering, pity the afflicted, shield the joyous and all for your love's sake."[1] For Folkwein and her people, this spiritual discipline became a lifeline.*

❖

Pastors, priests, and rabbis all reported initiating new ways of doing pastoral care in this crisis, figuring it out repeatedly as the pandemic wore on and on. They evaluated their lists of parishioners, recruited volunteers to make calls, sent scripts out, checked back on the callers to see who needed more attention. They dispatched teams to bring food or flowers. Rev. David Shirey, in Lexington, Kentucky, organized his entire congregation into groups of twelve families each and then deployed his Stephen Ministers, trained pastoral caregivers, to make weekly phone calls to church families to assess their needs. They all reported their findings back to him

---

1. Readings, Prayer at Compline, in *The Book of Common Prayer*, according to the use of the Episcopal Church.

so he could follow up. This method of organizing visitation was not uncommon. Many clergy independently devised systems for dividing the congregation into groups and then assigned these folks to lay leaders who took on the role of "shepherds." This method encouraged people to make social connections and provided a system for two-way communication. It proved to be an efficient way to identify who had prayer concerns, who was confused about how to get vaccines, and who had left town to live with a relative. In the faith communities where clergy devised this kind of shepherding system, it was easier to organize rides, assist with technology, organize drive-by birthdays, help with food deliveries, and many other things that were needed.

OFFICIATING AT FUNERALS

Deaths raised many questions and concerns for clergy. Funeral homes were allowing short services in chapels and common rooms. But these gatherings, when they did happen, were limited to immediate family and were necessarily short. Rabbi Carl Perkins found it stressful that he was not allowed out of his car at the cemetery until the burial was complete. It seemed so unnatural for him to remain cut off from his people in such moments. To make matters worse, many members of his congregation who lost loved ones could not sit shiva because no one was allowed to gather in each other's homes.

Rev. Julius Jackson reported that Rochester, New York, had been a close-knit community where funerals previously brought people together. But now, he identified a lingering sense of ungrieved loss as the pandemic took so many lives. With shortened funerals the grief felt incomplete because these services lacked so much: no choirs, no hugging, no large gatherings. Lots of people postponed their family funerals so long that eventually they simply let the time slip away without doing anything. The grief of the pandemic was punctuated by individual sorrow, but the widespread pathos in society is part of the story of this moment in history as many of the prayers, rituals, and words of comfort simply went unsaid.

The Perpetual Pivot

❋

In Susan's church one of our members was humble and unassuming despite being a pioneer and lead engineer in digital technology at companies in Boston. When he contracted COVID from a dialysis treatment, after months of carefully guarding his health, he was unable to visit with his wife and children and had to remain in a nursing home as the disease progressed. Eventually he went to the hospital to die, and his wife called us to tell us what was happening. Susan called his unit in the hospital and asked his nurse to put the phone to his ear. Listening to his uncertain breathing, she talked to him quietly, read from John's Gospel and said the Lord's Prayer along with a benediction. It did not seem like very much, given what he was going through. We could not tell his story in our sanctuary or honor his brave years of barrier-breaking accomplishments. But his wife called the next day to say how much she appreciated the phone call as the nurse had described it to her. He died within an hour of our conversation, and there was a sense that we were on holy ground that day.

❋

Rev. Amy Lignitz Harken, of Mattapoisett, Massachusetts, described the impact of these pastoral encounters, saying that prior to the pandemic the visible part of her ministry was the big stuff: the sermons in front of crowds or the eulogies delivered for someone in the community. But as the pandemic set in and stayed, it became the invisible parts of ministry that proved to be the vital stuff of her work. "So many visible things like passing the peace or the offering plates were put on hold while the most invisible aspects of ministry, like visiting at the window of someone who was sick or calling an elderly church member who she imagined would not get many interactions, was suddenly front and center."

4

Community Ministry Explodes

AS HAPPENED IN CITIES *around the world, when Boston businesses closed at the onset of the pandemic, the city was deserted in a matter of days. As rector of a church near the Boston Common, Rev. Pam Werntz realized the pandemic would be especially hard on the unsheltered people living near her church. Without access to water, public toilets, showers, or any way to ask for handouts or buy a cup of coffee, people who lived on the streets were virtually stranded. Werntz proposed that her church open its doors and offer unsheltered people a place to fill a water bottle, to sit inside, to take a nap, make a cup of tea, or charge a cell phone. Her vestry considered her suggestion seriously and then backed her, soon partnering with another downtown congregation. Together, the two downtown Episcopal churches trained volunteers and offered respite care six days a week.*

Werntz discovered this program made a big impact on the people living on the streets. That was expected, but then something unexpected happened for Werntz. It was as though her own faith had come alive at this moment. She took a risk initiating the program, because the fear of contagion, in some people's minds, made them nervous about those without shelter, as it was assumed that they would spread illness. In this crisis she developed the habit of saying, "Safety is not a gospel value." As it turned out, throughout the pandemic, no one that they knew of in the street population using their churches contracted COVID-19; they were startled and reported that somehow the program never seemed to spread the disease.

The third prong of religious leadership is prophetic witness. In the Bible, people identified as prophets had the reputation for speaking truthfully for God. Their pronouncements often highlighted the discrepancies between justice for the rich and the poor and became the conscience of the nation. The prophetic aspect of ministry is the work of the clergy in envisioning programs to assist the poor, to work for justice, and to motivate people to come to the aid of those who are struggling on life's uneven playing field. While prophetic leadership is always important, the COVID pandemic and the unequal distribution of resources it revealed in many communities convinced clergy to ramp up this work. For many, it was as though the pandemic issued a new call to the role as prophet. It was a call to expand the way they lived out their faith and many projects they undertook were radically new. Congregations of all sizes and in every state responded to the gaps in the social service networks that were exposed by the pandemic, and they addressed needs that had been lifted to an emergency level.

SOCIAL NEED EVERYWHERE IN THE PANDEMIC

Food shortages were a huge problem across the country both in urban and rural areas. When schools shut down and shifted to online classes, many children and young people who had relied on school meals every day for steady nutrition suddenly lacked enough food to eat. UNICEF reported that 370 million children worldwide were at risk for hunger in the pandemic due to schools closing.[1] Cities and towns all registered the far-reaching effects of losing school breakfasts and lunches. Led by their clergy, many faith communities stepped into the breach as thousands of volunteers began to

1. Krisberg, "COVID-19 Pandemic Fueling Rise in Child Hunger."

collect food, pack meals and organize food distribution sites on church parking lots and lawns. They set up grocery delivery systems and took prepared meals to schools for distribution to hungry families. Churches that had been providing monthly community meals before the pandemic were now distributing weekly grocery bags. Others were cooking meals or outsourcing food preparation to local restaurants in need of business.

During COVID a flurry of new programs sprang up to meet the enormous new needs. As the pandemic wore on and jobs were lost or relocated, many families also needed clothes, diapers, toiletries, and other basics. Clergy put tremendous energy into organizing coat drives, clothing drives, and ways to distribute toiletries and diapers safely. These were ambitious programs, and they had to be organized in such a way so as to prevent spreading illness. Volunteers had to be recruited and trained. It took hours to find food, cook it, and discover ways to package it safely. Clergy also envisioned clothing drives that allowed people to drop garments at the church safely, so volunteers could clean, package and redistribute them to needy members of the community. All these logistical challenges emerged in a society still trying to understand how the virus was spread.

As we marveled at the energy in the voices of the people we interviewed when they spoke about these new outreach efforts, we wondered whether clergy who had been frustrated by an inability to lead in the usual ways had made the decision, consciously or unconsciously, to leave their buildings and serve a wider population in innovative ways. Perhaps being barred from serving their people in worship and the usual programs led them to reach out to a wider audience, addressing the urgently pressing needs in their towns and cities.

Many faith leaders reported that these emergency relief programs gave them a heightened sense of purpose, and the work invigorated their congregation's sense of mission. Some found that serving the wider community was more fulfilling than they expected. The outreach programs transformed how they saw themselves and raised questions about their calling and their careers.

The Perpetual Pivot

For many, the crisis posed a faith imperative that caused them to reimagine their work in terms of prophetic action and to lead their congregations to chart new courses as well.

The pandemic also caused clergy to question *how* they did outreach in their community. With so many cards of modern life up in the air, ironically, the weight of this experience and the depth of need may have actually freed them to imagine whole new avenues of support for the poor. Some partnered with other non-profit groups. Some braved new paths led by the needs they saw all around them.

When the pandemic hit in Vermont, Rev. Kathleen Clark of East Arlington first thought she should retreat into the cocoon of her rural congregation and hide out, away from the wider community. Instead, she made a conscious decision to expand her church's welcome, and she did that by relying on her experience as a grant writer. She envisioned a program she called "Everyone Eats" in which the church purchased food from a different local restaurant each week, prioritizing farm-to-table local growers. Her church distributed meals to eighty families who drove through the parking lot for the pick-up. Soon the church expanded this project to target high schoolers who were hungry and distributed five thousand meals to teens. With awe in her voice, she described how her small church became known as "the face of hope" in their town.

❧

In another small congregation, in Western Connecticut, Rev. Robyn Gray enlisted faith leaders from the synagogue and seven local churches to sponsor a series of food drives. Together, they collected five tons of food and $20,000 in donations to feed local families. In the process the clergy found each other and developed strong bonds of friendship as they raised their profile as community leaders. They now have plans to sponsor a refugee family. This work also increased Gray's visibility in her town and brought many new members to her congregation.

❧

Often cited for her impact in her Cape Cod community before the crisis, Rev. Nell Fields credits the pandemic for being the catalyst to a more significant ministry than ever before. As the leader of the "little church doing big things," she believes the injustice laid bare in the pandemic spurred her congregation to reach out to strangers in new ways. Forced to let go of things she could not control, she led her church out into the community. The image she used for this new focus was the Promised Land Moment when you need to go in faith and hope so you can bring your people along with you. Many of Field's church programs like a favorite Giant Yard Sale had to be scrapped in the pandemic. But they pivoted to start a weekly feeding program to provide meals to neighborhood families, homeless people, and anyone in need—all by using local restaurants struggling for business. Each meal included a personal note. Fields and her people discovered they love feeding people!

❖

In Nebraska, Rev. Jim Keck led his congregation to work on reducing medical debt after learning that one in five Americans reported that their medical debt was aggravated by the pandemic. The church took money from its offerings to adopt someone in the community and pay off their debt. He sent a letter explaining what they had done and how their debt had been paid in full by First Plymouth Congregational Church. People who'd been helped called the church with tears in their voice to express a gratitude that words could hardly convey. This was the first of several initiatives at First Plymouth to reach out beyond the walls of their cathedral-like building. As they began to see strangers as neighbors, they hired a new young pastor to start an additional worship service in a local school auditorium. Through these efforts and as a result of the pandemic, the congregation's role in the city has been transformed from a leading sanctuary in the city to a people who reach out into the city to express their faith in community outreach. The church's new emphasis on looking outside its walls now guides the whole program in profound new ways.

The Perpetual Pivot

A RESORT VILLAGE ON THE COAST OF ALASKA AND ONE PASTOR WHO CHANGED IT

When the pandemic hit, Rev. Nico Reijns was a brand new pastor in a Methodist church in a small resort village on Alaska's Southern coast. As the business implications of the pandemic became clear, the CEO of the biggest resort employer called him. She was preparing to lay off seven hundred employees, and she wanted to talk to a pastor. She knew her actions would rock the community of 2,500. Reijns listened to the CEO and prayed with her. Then he did something that seemed natural to him but would have long-lasting implications for his work. He pledged to her that no one would go hungry. At the time, he couldn't have anticipated how this promise would change him or his ministry.

New to town, Reijns had already begun to see his church building as a natural hub on the Alaskan coast. From the start, he recognized that children in the area could not attend school online because the internet in the region was so spotty. So, he strengthened the church's Wi-Fi and turned the church hall into a hotspot. Elementary aged children gathered there daily to do online schooling. As they did, Reijn's vision of the church as a community space began to form, especially as people were then laid off.

Next, Reijns led the effort to assemble grocery bags for any family in need of food in the town. They mobilized volunteers and used the church building to pack the bags with meals donated by local restaurants. These efforts expanded beyond church volunteers hoping to make a difference to include a cohort of community folks not affiliated with any house of worship. Together, they forged a group of citizens determined to stop hunger in their village. In the spring of 2020 they served 267 families. Before long they were handing out as many as seven hundred bags of food a week and feeding an average of four hundred families monthly. Volunteers from all over town came forward. Many had no interest in religion but were committed to donating their time and large amounts of money to support this program at the church.

Community Ministry Explodes

As the feeding program and school internet site became fixtures in the community, Reijns began to wonder if he was being led to re-imagine his role in the village . What would it look like if he started to serve the town as well as the church? When he had first arrived, he had discovered the church, although located in a resort area with many expensive homes, was hard pressed to afford his salary and a parsonage. With the success of the grocery program for hungry families, he started to carve out a larger role for himself, not just as a spiritual leader but as a leader of community programs, which happen to be on church grounds. As the village started to re-envision the church as a community hub, so did the congregation. Before the pandemic, church leaders believed their job was to worship weekly, run youth groups, offer Sunday School, and fill committees. Now they saw the church as a faith community yoked to a non-profit community center. This community center could serve as both the action arm of the faithful congregation, and be a place that enables a wider group of volunteers to serve the village's needs.

In this new model for his ministry, Reijns is moving into the role of part-time pastor and part-time CEO of the community center. At our interview he was starting to write grant proposals for the community work, with an eye toward continuing to preach, teach, and pray at the church. In the vision he shared with the church, the non-profit would provide a food pantry, community garden, and emergency assistance. With a shared mission and shared leadership, the church and community center could become partners in serving the town, with a pastor who splits his time and draws his salary from both entities. If this new model is successful, it will make ministry affordable to the church and connect the community center to a steady stream of volunteers.

❧

When the clergy envisioned and led these outreach projects they were lauded for their efforts. Volunteers were eager to join, many welcoming the newfound sense of purpose after idle weeks at home. Few people disputed the importance of treating neighbors in need as children of God. In Rev. Werntz's church in Boston's

Back Bay, an innovative approach to serving the needs of people living on the street evolved out of the chaos of the pandemic as people of faith came to recognize that those without housing were struggling with their own particular needs as a result of the pandemic. Many people found purpose across the nation by serving others, and they credited their ministers with being the prophetic leaders who inspired them.

RACIAL JUSTICE AND POLITICS: A RECIPE FOR CONFUSION

The accolades that came to clergy for their leadership in establishing food distribution and clothing drives all too often disappeared when they took prophetic stances about racism in the summer of 2020. As the pandemic progressed into the summer, people charged with prophetic leadership could not ignore the racial injustice laid bare by the pandemic. At first clergy reported seeing discrepancies in healthcare and the way that COVID-19 was affecting people of color in greater numbers. It was hard to overlook the fact that people of color were often serving in greater numbers in careers that put them in danger on the front lines. People of color worked in nursing homes, public transportation, or other jobs that exposed them to the illness daily. Plus, when they got sick, they had poorer health outcomes and died at higher rates, often because they lacked access to good healthcare.

As the news media began to report on this phenomenon, the nation was then rocked by the news of the murder of George Floyd, a resident of Minneapolis who was killed by police on May 25, 2020. Dying at the hands of a police officer who knelt on his neck, for over nine minutes while Floyd lay handcuffed on the ground beneath the officer, Floyd's murder was captured on the cell phone of a teenager, Darnella Frazier. Her digital record went viral, shocking the nation with its sobering but riveting footage.

After centuries of unsolved murder cases where white people killed black citizens through lynchings, as well as police brutality that resulted too often in fatal injuries, why this one murder served as a wake up call is hard to pinpoint. Perhaps, in the pandemic, white Americans simply had more time to see this video. But perhaps they were especially horrified watching someone being strangled during a pandemic where the nation was in the grip of a virus that killed by attacking one's ability to breathe. That spring and summer the country embarked on a season of soul searching. Floyd's murder had raised the issue of racism, and the brutally violent way that people of color are treated, and took that conversation to a national level. Church communities have a biblical mandate to consider issues of justice. So, in the pandemic people of faith were swept up in the national debate about race and what to do about it.

Following the killing of George Floyd, clergy reported that they felt an overwhelming sense that they were being called to respond to racism in this country as people of faith charged to assume the role of prophetic thought leaders. They joined community marches to question and protest police overreach. They posted signs on church lawns saying "Black Lives Matter." They organized church-wide conversations about racism and led book discussions about racial bias. That summer, they preached more often about racial justice. In public displays of solidarity with clergy of color, white pastors showed up for public events.

In Washington D.C., Rev. Ellen Jennings organized Black Lives Matter rallies every weekend in the summer of 2020. Many other clergy-led groups who knelt on the church lawns for nine minutes and twenty-nine seconds, the amount of time Floyd was strangled, to help folks come to grips with how Floyd suffered. Jennings also started a social justice group to examine how her church was influenced by and perpetuated systemic racism. With few exceptions, the clergy connected the dots between the inequity in healthcare delivery revealed by the pandemic, Floyd's murder and systemic racism throughout American society.

Indeed many faith leaders led classes about internalized racism, using books on the topic[2] classes where white parishioners

---

2. The most commonly mentioned book we heard about that was used for these discussion classes in churches was *White Fragility: Why It's So Hard for*

came to grips with their own internalized racism for the first time. An overwhelming majority of the people in our project mentioned such book groups in the aftermath of national events, which provided a moment when church folks were ready to talk about race. In Dartmouth, Massachusetts, Rev. Emily Keller had dozens of people regularly showing up for a series of classes on racism. So eager were they, that next they asked for a class on anti-Semitism, and twice as many attended.

For some, their commitment as faith leaders went hand in glove with their commitment to preach about racial tensions. Talking about racism in 2020 felt like a spiritual imperative to many clergy. They took to the pulpit to make statements and preach about justice. In Decatur, Georgia, Rev. James Brewer-Calvert reported that although several families left the church as a direct result of his preaching, in large measure he found a robust audience hungry for progressive, anti-racist messages from his pulpit as he seized his prophetic authority. Similarly, Rev. Beth Gedert, from Delaware, Ohio, considered preaching a gift in the summer of 2020. "I felt it was easier to engage with edgier tropics during the pandemic, especially after the Floyd murder," she said. She felt her preaching improved because she had given herself permission to become bolder in the pulpit as she sensed an urgency to speak the truth as she saw it. "Woe to me if I don't address it." Another pastor said, "Without the pandemic we never would have thought about George Floyd, and we are not the church we once were. We've changed, and we've tried to embody a new message."

However, not all clergy felt emboldened. Some seemed less clear about their role as prophetic faith leaders than they had been when it came to feeding people. While those projects took time and energy, they were no-brainers for many clergy. Leading conversations about faithful responses to racial tension in our nation was much more complex, nuanced, and fraught with controversy.

Rev. David Shirey carved out a middle ground. He had been meeting with Black clergy weekly in Lexington, Kentucky, for some time and had developed deep friendships with them. But racial

---

White People to Talk about Racism by Robin DiAngelo.

tensions hit very close to home in his Kentucky congregation as the people were divided about a botched raid in March of 2020, when police in Louisville, an hour from Lexington, killed a young woman named Breonna Taylor when they fired blindly into her home. Coming just two months before Floyd was murdered in Minnesota, there was no clear consensus about whether to address police overreach or call for continued support of the police. Shirey's long-standing friendships with his clergy friends of color obligated him to show up for press conferences and to stand up for justice in her case.

But Shirey told us he felt a conflict between his commitment to his clergy friends and to some people in his congregation who were wary about any criticism of the police. So, he sustained criticism from people on both sides of the issue, those who expected him to condemn racial injustice and those who expected him to advocate for the police in Kentucky. Some questioned him for going too far in speaking about racism, while others leveled criticism for failing to say enough. It would be easy to be paralyzed in that atmosphere, but as a seasoned church leader he found a middle ground that worked for him and had empathy for recent seminary graduates who were new to ministry because they lacked the experience to trust their instincts. The balance he found enabled him to stay in dialogue with his Black clergy colleagues while grounding his sermons in the Bible readings in a way that avoided controversy.

Still others were vehement that mentioning politics in sermons was an abuse of their power, a temptation they had to resist, especially in an election year and a polarized nation. The racial strife in the country was potentially distracting. Rev. Brad Bergfalk felt it would have been a big mistake to get caught up in the "political craziness after the death of George Floyd," especially in his church where this topic was so controversial. For these clergy, their role as pastors eclipsed their responsibility as prophets, and they avoided discussing issues they felt would be divisive, such as racism or policing.

In Appleton, Wisconsin, Rev. Mary Bauer discovered that the challenge she faced was a political one, "how to bring people together from different sides and keep them together." She reported preaching plenty of sermons about white privilege, but they became controversial and people accused her of being an "outpost of the Democrats." She tried to emphasize that liberal theology is different from liberal politics, but the pandemic exacerbated the fault lines in the congregation. By this time in the pandemic some members were already convinced that closing the church was indicative of a liberal agenda. The whole experience emphasized for Bauer how important it was to be a non-anxious presence in the pulpit and as a lead pastor.

NEW PURPOSE AND OUTWARD FOCUS

From Alaska to Massachusetts the pandemic pushed faith leaders to envision a new role for themselves and their communities. As we interviewed religious professionals, what emerged was a sense that the pandemic provoked clergy to ask harder questions. There was a kind of "come to Jesus" quality in the air. Two separate trends contributed to this phenomenon. First, the crisis was deadly and costly and staggering in its long-term effects. As of this writing, in September 2023, COVID has caused 1.127+ million deaths, according to the World Health Organization in what has been for many Americans the most frightening and traumatic experience of their lives. Second, sustained periods of isolation and curtailed activity offered the space and time to ask these hard questions and ponder what the prophetic lessons from this experience might be. For many in our society this crisis opened a period of reflection on life's purpose and meaning, and religious leaders may be chief among them. After many months without the use of their church's real estate, many congregations re-envisioned those spaces as places of community gathering that could be used all week long.

Rev. Elizabeth Goodman served two small churches in a resort area in Western Massachusetts. One congregation served vacationers in the summer months but had a large group of parishioners from an adult mental health facility, both patients and clinicians, the rest of the year. Her second congregation sat in the center of a thriving town. Goodman used the pandemic to reevaluate the best way to lead two separate congregations and help them both reach their potential.

For the first congregation, after a lot of reflection, she encouraged this church to become a chapel connected to the mental health hospital nearby. Under the plan they'd continue to draw summer worshippers but serve year-round as a community space for workers and clients at the facility. As part of this new vision, Goodman phased out of her role as their pastor.

For the second church, Goodman used the pandemic to lead a conversation about how to transform its older building to become a community-gathering space in the historic downtown. Church members voted to renovate and create flexible space for a variety of functions, including worship. Goodwin decided she was needed and felt called to continue to serve this second church as it grows into a multi-purpose sacred gathering facility. The pandemic offered her a unique opportunity to be honest with both congregations about her assessment and then to patiently guide them to reassess their futures.

❈

In California, Rev. Loletta Barrett led her people to reimagine their Friends Meeting House as a gathering place for all faiths. Barrett believes that if "every room is not full, we are wasting space." They used the pandemic to imagine how to open their doors to new groups. Now they house a Friends School for kids on the autism spectrum, a community choir, an Orthodox Synagogue on Fridays, a Seventh Day Adventist Church on Saturdays, and a Mortuary Chapel for funerals all week long. Theirs is an ambitious model, but she has navigated the leadership of sharing space by explaining that the synagogue's ark of the covenant with its tree of life serves as a backdrop for all the congregations and is an example of how they can work together.

❈

The Perpetual Pivot

Coming as it did, after years of church decline, the COVID-19 pandemic served in many congregations, as a wake-up call. During the shutdown clergy were primed to step back, evaluate their options realistically, and ask hard questions. Suddenly, more options were on the table, and there was an openness to use the time to explore and re-think the mission of the congregation. Ironically, the severity of the crisis opened a door to new possibilities. Out of that kind of very basic reappraisal came some striking new visions for service and justice in many communities of faith.

5

Crisis Leadership
New Authority or Mutiny on the Bounty?

Rev. Bette McClure of Fairhaven, Massachusetts, has been leading her congregation on the South Coast of Massachusetts for twenty one years as senior pastor. When the pandemic began she closed the church building, as did all other South Coast ministers of UCC churches. Several of her church leaders, however, disagreed with her decision, saying, "The state of Massachusetts has no right to close us. We should reopen." Chairs of the Church Council and Property Committee along with the treasurer pressed to reopen. McClure researched advice from the denomination as well as the Center for Disease Control, but it was rejected by these lay leaders as emanating from liberal sources. A church survey was conducted and showed the congregation was split 50–50 on whether to remain closed in 2020. With help from some lay leaders, McClure found ways for people to occupy the sanctuary for Sunday services while wearing masks and sitting six feet apart. One member, however, refused to wear a mask. Lay leaders instructed McClure to call this member to remind her about the masking rule. The member responded with verbal abuse then demanded the Church Council call for McClure's resignation on the ground she was "unchristian." Others joined in calling for

McClure's resignation. The council supported the pastor in a vote of confidence. However, in the end, six prominent families, which included most of the lay leadership, left the church. In truth, this exodus was the fruit of a long-threatened leadership dispute that had lurked in the wings for years. The pandemic set in motion the perfect storm and a soul-wrenching time for McClure.

"*In my mind the sad part of this is that the people who left the church had been members from before the start of my ministry; some were lifelong members. Though I did not agree with their views, I valued them as members and was sorry to see them go. Plus, I worried about the effect of losing so many leaders. At this point one parishioner suggested that perhaps I should retire. In some ways I wanted to leave, but I refused to be run out.*"

The COVID-19 public health crisis pushed everyone to their limit. It raised questions about how to organize our lives, how to stay safe, how to educate children, and how to worship God. Every institution in our society faced queries about who was in charge of answering their questions or making decisions on our behalf. From the highest levels of government to the smallest county health department, people were thrown into a huge quandary. Who decides when we mask? Where can we go safely? How do we gather? Do we wash our groceries? Do we get vaccinated and how? The list was long. When the public questioned all these things, Dr. Anthony Fauci, Director of the US National Institute of Allergy and Infectious Diseases, who had served seven presidents, became an authority advising the public how to navigate these uncharted waters. For some, his advice was right up there with the Oracle at Delphi. But over time, his advice became controversial in an increasingly polarized society.

Clergy were not immune to this phenomenon of polarization. As leaders of churches, they were often the ones to decide whether and when to mask, how to conduct baptisms, weddings or funerals, how to collect money, and whether to visit the sick. Though they made all these decisions with the best intentions, it was difficult if not impossible to rely on traditional decision-making processes. While they had come to rely on the advice of lay leaders before the pandemic, now it was hard to find all those leaders or to create forums to discuss their options, and often there was no time. Before long the clergy discovered that every one of these decisions could prove controversial or the fodder for church debate.

The pandemic revealed one of the long-standing issues in this unique and unusual profession. Many clergy find that they are expected to take responsibility for making decisions but not always given the authority to make those decisions stick. Congregations may hold their leaders in high esteem and expect them to make tough decisions, but those same congregations can also review and critique decisions without seemingly negating the clergy's authority to make them. As a result, for many ministers, being asked to make a tough decision can feel like a trap. It can feel like they will easily be second-guessed, or their professional expertise may be discredited. This tension between the congregation's expectations for leadership and decision-making and the subsequent decision to revoke that authority is not new.

One of the best examples of this tension did not arise from our interview data but from the religious history of the early 1700s, exactly three centuries ago. In 1721, Cotton Mather was a minister in the colony of Massachusetts when people experienced the worst outbreak of smallpox. That year, over 50 percent of the colonists became ill—5889 out of 11,000 residents in Boston; of those, 844 died. The 1721 wave of disease was only one of a series of seven waves or variants of this illness that struck the colonies in those years. At that time the Chinese had already been inoculating people for smallpox for seven hundred years. They were accustomed to exposing people to dried smallpox scabs so they would develop natural immunity from exposure to a less severe form of the illness. This is the principle behind inoculation. The idea proved so successful that it spread through Turkey and parts of Africa, but innoculations were not known to New Englanders.

It was Mather who is largely credited with introducing inoculation to the colonies. He had learned about it from his slave, Onesimus, who was born in West Africa where he had been inoculated himself. When smallpox spread from an infected sailor on a ship that arrived in Boston Harbor in April 1721, Mather reached out to Boston physicians with what he had learned from Onesimus, suggesting people should be inoculated with a small amount of pus from a smallpox patient. The idea was so controversial that only one doctor agreed to try what seemed to other physicians like a dangerous experiment. In an atmosphere of fierce debate, Mather inoculated his own family, but the general populace remained skeptical. At the height of the controversy someone threw a bomb through the window of the Mather home. It did not detonate but the note attached cursed the reverend saying, "I'll inoculate you with this, a pox to you."[1]

The question of how to find the authority to lead in a crisis was one of the biggest fulcrums on which the clergy sought to balance their ministry. Many clergy felt that they were doing their best in the midst of unprecedented stress only to discover that they were at the center of a crisis of leadership and being questioned at every turn. When the pandemic crisis caused them to assume outsized roles, believing they had no choice or that congregational safety demanded it, their hard decisions came at great personal cost. Like Mather three centuries ago, many clergy today proved to be ahead of their communities, and some of their best ideas were scorned or rejected, even when history would prove them right.

How clergy felt about the pandemic, indeed how they felt about their work as faith leaders, often hinged on whether or not they believed their people recognized their efforts or extended them the benefit of the doubt. When stressors hit and leaders felt supported by their congregations, though things were difficult, they managed to prevail. But when criticisms of their decisions turned into controversy and people lost respect for the clergy, faith leaders grew frustrated and started to question whether their leadership efforts were worth it. In those congregations where the clergy were the target of criticism, the stress grew exponentially.

---

1. "Cotton Mather." Mather (1663–1728) was one of the most influential Puritan ministers and writers in New England. He was also known for his scientific research and as an author of forty books.

Change is always hard in faith communities. The pandemic took congregations down a long path of continuous change, careening at new speeds. Congregants became tired, uncertain, and anxious. All the new safety protocols, combined with different ways to worship, meet in groups, collect money, and so forth sent shock waves through many churches and synagogues. Plus, in this emergency, decisions had to be made quickly, and as a result, old patterns of decision-making were impossible. Church offices were closed. Meetings, when they happened, were online. Clergy who were used to building consensus by button-holing key decision makers could not see them in person to read their body language or other subtle cues. Clergy were often the sole strategists, leaving lay leaders feeling sidelined. While it would be naïve to think that religious leaders don't always have a hand on the scale when important decisions are made, successful pastors and rabbis are often subtle and precise in exerting their influence. Now, there was no time for subtlety. It felt like survival required decisive action. Congregations relied on them to do this, but often there was backlash.

NAMING ANXIETY

Rev. Kristen Heiden of Marietta, Georgia, heard so many opinions, ideas, and laments, it was hard to know which way to turn: "We are all vaccinated; we don't need masks"; "The kids are sick of online activities; let's start religious education in person"; "Let's go to one service and all stay together"; "We miss the two services we used to enjoy. Why did you do that?" She said, "I had to ask myself what is my role and calling here? What do they need to hear from me?" While juggling safety advice from all quarters, including the Centers for Disease Control, the United Methodists, and the congregation, no matter how hard she tried to keep a clear focus, it was stressful. But, she said, a lot of church member's advice came from anxiety, and anxiety is contagious.

❧

The clergy who could step away from the conflict in their churches and see the anger as fear and hear the frustration as anxiety had ways to analyze the conflict they faced. That was the first step in recognizing that while they might feel like they were the focus of these congregational disputes, in truth, they were not responsible for the conflict and often felt as helpless as everyone else. However, the real feat for clergy, and it took a great deal of emotional maturity and wisdom, was managing their own anxiety while absorbing that of others. One pastor reported seeing more mental health issues than ever. She had to remind herself that her parishioners were in pain and then endeavor to listen. That simple act diffused the unrest, especially to the extent she could communicate that these people had been heard.

Perhaps the secret to McClure's staying power in her church was her ability to weather the storms of conflict. Somewhat to her surprise, once the combative church leaders had left the church, the congregation experienced a whole new flowering of positive leadership. She reported that the pandemic has made her more honest. It has given her more insight into the church conflict she had faced for some time, and how it affected her, making it hard to be a steady leader. But the way she weathered this extraordinary level of conflict, she believes, has made her a better pastor.

CONFUSION ABOUT SMALL BUSINESS MODEL OR CHARITY MODEL

In some congregations the seeds of conflicts were sewn from the beginning, but they really grew as the pandemic wore on. Fault lines in many churches are formed between those who want to run the church like a small business and those who believe the congregation should model a higher level of kindness and consideration in treating employees. When congregations realized they were paying people who could not do their work in the church building, debates swirled in many congregations about whether to continue paying them. People argued that religious communities should retain staff as a way to support loyal employees and find work for them. Others wanted to let them go in order to save money. Lots of clergy reported that they had applied for and received government payroll assistance in the form of Payroll Protection Program (PPP) loans, but that process was lengthy and involved. A number of clergy confided that they quietly found work for their custodians, assigning them to cleaning projects and long-deferred upkeep and renovations to keep them gainfully employed.

The debate between these two models for running congregations is often unnamed and largely unconscious in communities of faith. Some churches straddle the fence making some decisions from a business model while others are decided with an eye to justice in personnel policy. But the ambivalence about whether to be a business or a charity was laid bare in the pandemic, though rarely acknowledged as such. Some people argued vehemently about church administration issues because they were already experiencing stress in other areas of life and felt adamant that their faith community should remain predictable, complete with all the unexamined assumptions they brought to it.

SWEET SPOT—RELYING ON THEIR CORE STRENGTHS

One leadership trend that emerged from our interviews was that faith leaders, when pushed to the wall by unresolved debates or administrative conundrums, began to rely on their most basic ministry instincts. The born administrators created plans and coping strategies. The mystics at heart led from a place of spiritual depth. People who began as community organizers reached out into the community to form alliances. Former church planters like Rev. Patrick Wrisley of Fort Lauderdale, Florida, challenged the staff at the church where he was lead pastor to change its leadership style to become more flexible and adapt quickly to each new challenge. That approach which is basic for church planters is rarely used in well-established multi-staff churches, but it proved an effective approach in the crisis. Plus, Wrisley felt most comfortable operating with this approach. In similar ways Rev. James Brewer-Culvert from Decatur, Georgia, played to his strengths as a community organizer. Following the playbook from Saul Alinsky (1909–72), political activist, community organizer, and theorist from Chicago, he used networking skills to bring people together by deploying deacons to organize groups of ten families each to distribute food and to tend the church gardens. As he felt most comfortable wearing his organizer's hat, it became most comfortable in the crisis.

Rev. Stuart Spencer of Moorestown, New Jersey, was new to his church in 2020 and found himself leading a contentious governing board. Troubled by the fierce debate, he introduced a way to lead based on Scripture. A Bible scholar himself, he cemented his authority and dispelled a lot of anxiety by developing a leadership program based on Scripture. He developed a set of Scripture themes with accompanying verses for every month of the program year. Then he encouraged every committee and social group to begin meetings reading and reflecting on these Scripture passages, which united his people. Spencer preached a set of sermons that coordinated these Bible lessons, giving them focus and casting a vision for the congregation. In this way his reliance on Scripture sent a message to his staff and his entire congregation that they could trust God in this crisis, no matter what happened.

❦

Clergy who felt trusted were less invested in pleasing people or second guessing themselves.

Rev. Melanie Enfield from Newington, Connecticut, reported that she had to work through her own exhaustion as a daughter who lost her father, as a mother with two young adults at home, and as a pastor who missed the energy she relied on from a live audience when she preached. The lesson she learned as a church leader during the pandemic was that her own identity could not be so closely tied to the success of things in her congregation. Something in that shift freed her to try many new things; she rarely heard anyone say, "This is not the way we do things." Her people seemed confident in her leadership as she built an atmosphere of more mutual understanding. Careful not to pretend to have the answers, Enfield led by asking,

"Who is God calling us to be in this moment?" She did not assume that she would be able to answer that question but was honest about the ways that she too was seeking more faith herself. When she took an online class, "Painting for Non-Painters," she found it so meaningful that she invited the artists to do a retreat at her church. It was all part of her overarching vision to offer ways for God to use creativity to replenish people's spirituality. The retreat was successful and served as a good way to encourage people to follow Enfield's lead and engage in their own personal exploration. Through her leadership and example she tried to invite her people to engage in an exploration in this crisis. Throughout the experience whether she was asked about the use of the church kitchen, or how to start a new mission initiative, she framed her response with the question, "Who are we called to be?"

❀

Every crisis brings both challenge and possibility. COVID-19 was no exception. While this crisis was overwhelming for many clergy, it was also a fertile ground for new ideas, often born of necessity. As a result many clergy asked new questions about their roles and what was effective leadership. In some cases, the crisis gave birth to whole new initiatives that proved to have lasting implications.

RELIGIOUS EDUCATION

Reaching families with small children was hard, especially as children's vaccines were unavailable for two years into the pandemic. However we heard many stories of creative efforts to keep children and youth included. Clergy sent home kits with Bible readings and crafts for families to do together. They invited kids to share videos and pictures about their experience of faith. Rev. Ruth Shaver's congregation created a scavenger hunt based on the question "Where do you find God?" Next, Shaver preached a sermon series on Exodus and produced a five-part video on the story.

❀

The Perpetual Pivot

In Leonia, New Jersey, Rev. Leah Fowler created "Church in a Box" for her families. Each box included a model church they could cut out and put together, a communion table with cork legs, as well as little cloths in various liturgical colors. With it, kids set up their own sanctuaries at home. She included cards with the Ten Commandments, a book of devotions and other curriculum. Her church filmed a clip of Fowler dancing with the kids in the parking lot. She was so committed to including children in worship that every service featured children reading Scripture or playing music. On Christmas Eve the church had an online service where one hundred families seemed to pass a candle from one Zoom box to another. Her efforts were so well-received that the church attracted new families and added members at the height of the pandemic.

❧

When they could navigate the safety restrictions and feel confident about their authority, clergy created many new vibrant programs. In the warmer weather, church camps and vacation Bible schools flourished on lawns and under tents. More visible to people driving by, these efforts were so successful that churches are making outdoor religious education a permanent feature when weather allows. Even with this renaissance of children's programs many clergy admitted they were discouraged at the way the pandemic made it hard to attract children and youth. Breaking the Sunday morning routine for eighteen months proved to be a big disruption for many families. We heard stories about successful programs for children and youth but often they were new initiatives. In continued conversations with clergy, the challenge to attract young families is an ongoing concern. It may prompt religious leaders to develop many more imaginative approaches outside the box of the "Sunday School Model."

MEMBERSHIP

During the pandemic the general population became more fluid. Many people were in transit, seeking refuge in homes of relatives, staking out new territory, moving to remote locales to weather the crisis. All these people in spontaneous motion meant the clergy faced the new hurdle of finding everyone. For faith communities, contact information became critically important, but many people left town without leaving much of a trail. The issue seemed larger than the difficulty of finding parishioners, though that loomed large throughout the crisis.

In addition, families confined at home for months went "church shopping" online. Many grew loyal to new preachers. While clergy enjoyed this surge of interest, they also admitted how confusing it was to connect to the online audience, to learn their names, to understand what they were seeking—all the normal things you might expect to do with a new visitor who came in-person. This was also true for people seeking classes online. Rabbi Carl Perkins from Needam, Massachusetts, was delighted to report that his Torah class included people studying in New York, Northern England, and South Africa. But how do you incorporate such a group into a synagogue community? This sense of flying blind was again reawakened.

In normal times, faith communities put stock in their census data—worship attendance, class rolls, and contribution lists—as this data provides a reliable snapshot for leadership decisions. The data is used to determine the size of staff, how many to expect in worship, and how to project program needs. While there is no standard way to take the census in a congregation, and all the systems leave room for subjective decisions about exactly what constitutes a member, faith communities rely on consumer interest, so clergy rely on this data.

Many clergy worried that it was increasingly hard to find good data at all. This was a topic of concern in almost every interview. Keeping track of members on the rolls is a challenge in normal times, but in the pandemic it called for exhaustive detective work as congregants joined other churches online, moved across the country or lost interest in religion altogether.

Among the outliers who created new ways to connect with people who surfaced online was Rev. Hollie Woodruff of Richmond, Virginia. She appointed "web deacons" and set up membership criteria for her online crowd. After two services, her web "deacons" asked visitors for an e-mail address so Woodruff could invite them to a Zoom meeting to get acquainted. As a result Woodruff welcomed a cadre of new members who joined virtually. Rev. Paul Davis from Greensboro also reported that his church had eased membership protocols in the pandemic and were welcoming people with virtual rituals. In our survey 15 percent of clergy welcomed new members during the pandemic. In some cases like the Buffalo, New York, church served by Rev. Nancy Rosas, they continued to grow the congregation. However, others worried about how to maintain a robust membership. The migration to virtual and hybrid forums, which was starting before COVID but accelerated by the crisis, raises the question of whether basic assumptions about membership are relevant or need to be adjusted in the future.

FINANCES—HOW DO WE PAY FOR EVERYTHING?

In our earliest interviews, conducted in August and September 2020, clergy reported being worried about finances. Without in-person worship, there was no time set aside every week to encourage people to give financially and no ritual for collecting money. However, as the pandemic wore on, faith leaders reported meeting their budgets for 2020, in some cases exceeding revenue projections. Electronic giving and online gifts balanced their budgets handily. It seemed people had rallied in this crisis and responded with new levels of generosity. But the pandemic did raise more fundraising issues. When weekly worship was the standard, especially in the latter part of the twentieth century, collecting revenue at the weekend worship services made sense and proved reliable. But recently, with declining church attendance, "passing the plate" is a less dependable way of meeting financial needs and leaves churches vulnerable to a cash flow crunch. Prior to the pandemic, many congregations had already begun touting online giving to address the cash flow issue. The pandemic just accelerated this shift. Clergy were vocal about the benefits of this change, recommending the budgeting benefits of knowing how much to expect monthly.

Faith communities have relied on remarkable levels of generosity over the decades and been the envy of nonprofit fundraisers. Every non-profit that asks contributors to "make a pledge" is using the church's playbook. However the key to vibrant church fundraising is based on the personal connections that are nurtured through shared experiences like breaking bread sacramentally or literally at community suppers. One of the trends to watch is whether changes in attendance also bring a long-term corrosive effect on the financial stability of these religious institutions.

For now, the pattern of weekly in-person appeals has proven successful. Though most churches eliminated the passing of plates in the crisis, and suspended it even when in-person worship resumed due to concerns about spreading the virus. However as they returned to the pews, people were eager to restore tradition, and many have reinstated this practice. Whatever method of payment is encouraged, time set aside to remind people about the spiritual benefits of giving can be both vitally important to the spiritual health of the church, as well as the bottom line.

LASTING LESSONS AND NEW INITIATIVES

In Falmouth, Massachuestts, Rev. Nell Fields used this moment to reflect on how to be a more effective church leader. Restructuring her leadership model, she formed micro-groups, assigned work to them, and trusted their decisions. This shift from committees to short-term task groups made it easier to recruit volunteers and delegate leadership. She hired a trainer to teach the congregation how to use small leadership groups more effectively. All these changes have transformed her job and how her congregation operates. She credits the crisis for enabling her to try this.

❖

Though Field's was a rare example, the pandemic brought the opportunity to spark new conversations about how to organize more effectively. It offered churches the chance to examine their volunteer expectations. It brought with it enough disruption to provoke some authentic questioning about the models for leadership many churches use that are based on a time when families had more flexibility in the evenings for volunteering and more room in their schedules overall. The pandemic experience might offer congregations a wake-up call to reevaluate the roles of their officers or boards. It might provide the impetus to reconsider how best to use the skills and gifts of the clergy as they coordinate leadership with lay leaders. However, the key to whether this evaluation happens or not is based on how congregations treat the pandemic. If they regard it as an aberration, a dreadful interruption from which they need to move on as quickly as possible, then any lessons in this experience may be lost. However, if faith leaders see the pandemic as a gift disguised as a crisis, perhaps they can ask the harder questions that might offer new insights about new paths for religious leadership, going forward into this new century.

6

The Toll on Clergy

IN THE AUTUMN OF 2022, Rev. Rebecca McElfresh of Sahuarita, Arizona, embarked on a much-needed sabbatical, a time of rest, prayer, spiritual reconnection, and, hopefully, restoration. During this time, she realized she was carrying the weight of so many worries after the pandemic. As she prayed about her strong feelings about what she had been through, she felt her soul drawn to a wrestling match with God, much like Jacob had in Gen 32:24–28. This feeling culminated for her in a labyrinth at Ghost Ranch, a Presbyterian retreat center in New Mexico. She writes:

"As I started the path, however, I was distracted by my feeling of being off balance, nearly tripping several times on the rocks that bordered the path. I heard the Spirit's voice, like a quiet ping, 'Let it go.' I realized in that moment that my backpack was weighing heavily on my shoulders and I threw it to the ground. As I regained my sense of balance, I recognized the metaphor it represented. Again, I heard the Spirit say, 'stay where you are.' I knew the message came because I had been struggling with my call to ministry, as many other pastors had during the pandemic. I felt my heart say to the Spirit, 'Okay, but you have to show me how.' With that I arrived at the center of

the labyrinth. There I sat down on a large rock to rest. A honeybee arrived shortly after I did, and she seemed determined to be in my space. I don't swat at bees. I usually walk away. However, this time I just gently tried to encourage her to move along. But she did not leave and instead parked herself right in front of my nose so that we were looking at each other eye to eye. I waited and waited, but still she remained. Then a third message came to me, 'I see you.'

McElfresh continued, "Suddenly, I felt seen, understood, and affirmed. At that moment I knew God was with me and would stay with me in the weeks ahead, as I tried to follow the Spirit's urging to find a new direction in my ministry."

The stories the faith leaders told us were much more than stories about clergy doing a job. Clergy like McElfresh spoke eloquently about the toll the pandemic took on them personally. Men and women whose lives had been upended by grief and change described burdens too heavy to carry indefinitely. These were people who got sick themselves, who lost family members and watched the fabric of their faith communities ripped by conflict that no level of expertise could appease. They were people of conscience, heartsick at societal storms that could not be easily calmed. Pastors, raw with all they had seen and done, began to question their original call to ministry. Our interviews revealed a human backdrop of personal grief mixed with a bedrock determination to serve others. Their deep humanity made the efforts they described all the more heroic.

One minister spoke about returning from her first maternity leave. A new pastor she had hoped to share all the infant's milestones that year with her people, but found, instead, she had to wait and wait and then wait some more to even introduce the baby. Finally, when her daughter was two, she could be vaccinated and meet the parish. No parishioners enjoyed her early smiles or watched her toddle across hallways. While this disappointment is not enormous, and many pandemic babies were quite sheltered in the first months of life, it speaks to plenty of dreams deferred.

In 2020 another minister had just assumed the role of Senior Pastor of a large Methodist church, a plum position for any clergyperson and a special honor for a young woman. She approached this position assuming she would need to prove herself, especially in the beginning. She was also the mother of a four-year-old and a six-year-old. When the pandemic began her children suddenly needed to be homeschooled. It took all her energy to manage both her personal and her professional responsibilities. Though she was an experienced runner, used to exerting herself, the pandemic pushed her to her limits. In such a new assignment, she was uncertain how much she could share with her flock about her weariness, fearing they would doubt her ability to do the job.

Many felt torn between family needs and church responsibilities. Even those who were expert at juggling other people's needs had to take multi-tasking to a whole new level. They hosted young adults who had moved home, tended to aging parents in declining health, and nursed spouses sick with COVID. Many monitored the well-being of several generations, managing full houses of children and in-laws, all while navigating the unfolding complexities of church life, preparing inspiring sermons and inventing meaningful worship experiences. These ministers also lost mothers and fathers. They suffered the same losses as those they served and often they too had to mourn without saying a final goodbye. The people drawn to ministry are open-hearted by nature, and in this crisis they opened their homes as safe harbors for family members. We found a number of clergy were hosting multiple generations and handling their own anxieties while finding the strength to support everyone around them.

Six months into her new assignment as the Senior Minister of an active United Methodist Church in Linworth, a suburb of Columbus, Ohio, Rev. Anna Guillozet faced the challenge of leading her new congregation through the start of the COVID pandemic. Initially, she prioritized the church staff and preschool run by the church because together they employ fifty full-time workers and provide child care for many essential workers in the area. Guillozet studied state regulations and became an expert on healthcare requirements because she felt a great deal of pressure as so many people relied on the daycare program. For her, the additional responsibility she rarely talked about was managing her own anxiety as a person who had grown up with asthma and knew firsthand the visceral fear of being unable to breathe. In the spring of 2020 she also cared for her father who was waiting for a liver transplant. Starting in 2021, he moved in with her, living with her family for the last nine months of his life. In addition, Guillozet wanted to be an emotional support for her husband, who faced his own stressors as a county public health commissioner receiving death threats because of the masking policies he instituted. Guillozet shouldered all of these responsibilities while proving that she could lead a large church successfully for the first time in her career.

❖

An experienced multitasker Rev. Melanie Enfield was a senior minister of her church in Newington, Connecticut, a mother of two young adults, a thoughtful wife, and the daughter of an elderly dad. She knew how to take care of her family and her church simultaneously, but the pandemic pushed her on so many new emotional levels. Perhaps it was not the multitasking but the lack of connection or feedback from her people that proved, in the end, to be the greatest strain. She was so capable at multitasking because she thrived on connecting with folks, and that was missing in this crisis. Enfield reported that her father-in-law was living in a memory care unit and died in April 2020 without her or her husband there. Seven months later her own father died of COVID. Meanwhile, she nursed her son who was home that spring after orthopedic surgery, and helped navigate her daughter's return from Guatemala when the US borders were closing in the early weeks of the pandemic. As she began to preach to her empty sanctuary, she said, "There was a level of exhaustion from leading in this crisis that derived from giving so much and getting so few of the responses that I was used to in-person, responses that had sustained my energy in the past."

❖

At the height of the pandemic, exhaustion took over as many faith leaders shouldered more and more of the load in their congregations, their families, and the wider communities in which they served. When technology failed, clergy begged or borrowed equipment. When volunteers lost interest, clergy filled the gap. When staff resigned, clergy stepped into the breach. When congregations lost in-person connections, clergy invented new programs. When community members went hungry, clergy pledged to feed them. As the pandemic progressed, they kept on keeping on, navigating the rapid succession of pivots, each change bringing a new set of adaptations and stressors. Even those who had been energized by early successes or opportunities for creativity, sagged under the unremitting weight of responsibility. With no end in sight, many struggled to keep their spirits up, to stay engaged in their work and to press on. Several people we spoke to became ill with COVID-19 themselves, and a few were hospitalized with long illnesses.

As we compiled and analyzed these stories of widespread emotional exhaustion, we recognized that people attracted to this profession came to this calling, in part, because they had natural skills and aptitude for caring for others. Yet the load of responsibility that they carried in normal times grew exponentially when the pandemic got under way. Like the vicar in Geraldine Brooks' novel about the plague in the seventeenth century, these modern clergy monitored the sick, reached out to the lonely, wrote messages of hope, and cast a vision through sermons and podcasts. But they did not stop there. They organized ways to ensure that the whole community had enough food, clothing, and shelter. In this crisis they became modern examples of what it means to live in harmony, where neighbors share with strangers and no one is forgotten. They assumed an outsized role in their communities and in their families because of those very skills. As they widened the circle of their own flock to include whoever was in need, they expanded their influence in the community, but none of this was easy. The fact that they aspired to do it at all is a remarkable achievement. Over time, however, they depleted their own resources and began to run on empty.

What made the most difference to many of these men and women was being seen and having places where they could talk about what they were going through. Clergy with a support group found it to be a key coping mechanism. Just as the honeybee on Rebecca McElfresh's nose brought a sign of affirmation that her struggle had been recognized, clergy did better when they could give voice to their feelings and find someone was listening. But that took time. It took time for most congregations to recognize how stressed their leaders were becoming. Many faith leaders were not accustomed to sharing their own needs publicly, so it did not come naturally to be open about their struggles.

❊

In East Woodstock, Connecticut, Rev. Sue Foster ramped up her outreach efforts and produced more blogs under her handle "Fostering Your Faith," but she found the workload in the pandemic unrelenting, and it was hard to keep her own spirit and energy up. Even when she added additional hours of spiritual direction for herself, she found everything tiring. Eventually Foster got sick with COVID and was hospitalized for five days, reporting that she never felt so sick. When that happened her congregation took care of her husband and her son. After she was discharged from the hospital the congregation was generous about allowing her time to recuperate and continued to send meals every day for months. As she returned to work she knew she still had to pace herself, but given all her absences she wondered about whether she should take a grant she'd earned for a sabbatical that following summer. The church won her loyalty when they recognized how exhausted she was and insisted she take it. Foster spent the first month of sabbatical resting before taking a trip to Alaska.

❊

When congregations were generous and understanding, clergy felt seen and heard. It made their effort worthwhile. And many church members recognized the efforts of their leaders and the toll of the pandemic on them. Their notes and e-mails conveyed genuine appreciation. Many heard messages such as "Thanks for getting us through this pandemic"; "Thanks for keeping us all together"; "We appreciate all you have done to be the church for us." Many clergy reported that these heartfelt messages were what sustained them. They reminded the clergy of the wells of deep affection that had prompted their initial devotion to these people. Their struggles and their work meant something.

SURVIVAL STRATEGIES

In the spring of 2020, when clergy recognized that the pandemic was not a sprint but a marathon, many became proactive in establishing new goals for self-care. Realizing that their stress levels were building they set up schedules for sleep, hiking, yoga, running, prayer, and family time. It was clear to them that effective leadership required new levels of self-discipline. Rev. David Shirey in Lexington, Kentucky, preached a set of sermons on his fourfold philosophy for self-care. Each sermon described one part of his daily self-care regimen, a program that included prayer, reading, nurturing friendships, and exercising. He found it made such a difference in his own life that he wanted to model it and talk openly about the benefits of a proactive plan for self-care.

When the pandemic began Rev. Lucia Lloyd from Bowmanville, Ontario, worked especially hard adding online classes and additional prayer services. But she also prioritized journaling, daily hikes at noon, vacation travel, and healthy meals. She quickly recognized that without self-care, she simply could not care for others in the ways the situation demanded.

During the pandemic Rev. Dawn Adams went through a health scare in Brimfield, Massachusetts. As a pastor, she felt much more aware of her health and a heightened awareness that life is fragile. She told her church council that she needed to be very intentional about that. She started to hike regularly each day and eat more healthy meals. After ten months of that routine she had lost weight and was healthier. Adams also knew she needed clergy companions. So she started her own support group and it proved to be a lifeline.

Clergy support groups were game-changers for a lot of people. Rev. Laura Folkwein in Bozeman, Montana, sang the praises of a similar group in her state. They met to share challenges, ask for advice, and pray together. It was a group she gladly drove many miles to attend in person. In Pittsburgh, Rev. Randy Bush started a support group for senior pastors in his presbytery. It provided a unique place to brainstorm ideas, troubleshoot problems, and find the support he needed and needed to share. Forums where people could be honest about their questions or failure, get frank advice, find affirmation, or get new ideas made a huge difference.

The families of clergy can often feel like the church is a higher priority than they are. But the pandemic reinforced the need to balance mind, body, soul, family, and church causing many clergy to reexamine their priorities. They set aside time for family vacations, spontaneous recreation, hiking, games, movie nights, cooking together and doing home projects. Now some of this happened because so many youth and kids were home from school, but clergy mentioned the gift the pandemic gave them of renewed closeness to their children. They also resolved to avoid getting so swamped with work that they sacrificed their family time after the crisis.

Several clergy mentioned that the pandemic led to an enriched prayer life that fed their souls. Initially turning to prayer for spiritual nurture, Rev. Nell Fields in Falmouth, Massachusetts, was surprised to discover her faith really deepened in the pandemic. She decided to use the time to emulate the mystics for one year. Praying every day in a disciplined way resonated for her and helped her be more resilient and more centered as a leader.

❧

In Moorestown, New Jersey, Rev. Stuart Spencer viewed the pandemic as a call to deeper devotion. He referred to the way the Bible depicts crises like this as a call to repentance, and wondered how to lead his people in a sacred response to COVID. For many years he had prayed every morning, but in this crisis he was inspired by a group from a mission project in Kenya to try a new kind of "fasting prayer." The African people asserted that fasting was key to their spiritual vitality. Spencer began fasting for twenty-four hours each week, abstaining from eating food from Wednesday night's supper until *Thursday's*. *He believes this change has deepened his prayer life, grounded his leadership, and transformed his sense of religious authority.*

RESIGNING, RETIRING AND MOVING ON

We are still evaluating the cost of this experience on religious professionals, but from the beginning it proved to be considerable and ongoing, with no end in sight. Statistics on church leadership indicate that over 40 percent of the clergy found that the pandemic pushed their professional tolerance to the limit. At first, we attributed this to those stories about instances of bad member behavior in churches, protracted debates about masking, and bruising disputes with lay leaders who were angry at being unable to exert their former influence. However the stories about the emotional toll may point to a larger erosion of trust in some congregations. The kind of intense conflict that arose during the pandemic may stem from a deep-seated confusion in many congregations about the role of religious leaders. To work that hard and then be questioned by people who could not know their trials was, for some, the final straw.

The peculiar balance of clergy influence without corresponding authority, somewhat workable in normal times, became untenable. In some places the leadership model just broke down. The intense conflict we heard about was so disturbing that many clergy went into search and moved to new congregations, while others retired earlier than expected during the pandemic. Clergy who had tolerated being second-guessed for years suddenly felt the unfairness of it in new ways.

It should be noted that no congregation we learned about had granted clergy emergency executive powers in the pandemic. While there is precedent for that in state and federal government emergencies, none of these religious communities suspended their bylaws or constitution to allow their clergy the widest possible latitude. That might have addressed the imbalance that occurred in many churches. At the height of the pandemic sacred spaces were locked for many months, and the clergy reinvented their jobs to lead their faith communities. While leading in this emergency was an adjustment, some clergy grew to appreciate the freedom they had to make decisions when it was hard to consult lay leaders. But in 2021 as those leaders returned to their churches in person, they expected to pick up where they had left off almost two years earlier. They expected to be consulted on decisions, as they had been before COVID. However, in the interim period, many clergy had adopted new procedures and expectations. The clergy had traveled whole new roads without them. Plus when they did return in person eager to restore normality, many congregants did not have an accurate memory of how things had been done eighteen months prior. Yet the emotional pull to "get back to normal" and desire to insert their influence came with pent up vehemence. While many clergy weathered the crisis, it was the aftermath or reentry negotiations that proved even more acrimonious.

The pandemic prompted changes in many careers. Among our fifty-three interviews, five clergy changed settled positions, four were interim pastors and moved to new interim positions, and six retired, with one retiring to become an interim for a total of 28 percent. Many of them told us they simply could not stay where they were, attributing the problems they faced to a poor fit for them, a fact highlighted by the pandemic. Though finding a new congregation meant interviewing online and moving without seeing the house or church or leaders in person, the clergy who made these transfers felt driven. Their level of dissatisfaction was so high they were certain they had to move on.

One pastor from the Midwest started at a new church in 2018, but he left much earlier than he anticipated to accept a position as a pastor 2000 miles away. He said members of the first church were not convinced COVID was dangerous, and their debates about holding worship grew acrimonious. The pastor lost a family member to COVID, so his family was quite nervous about the mysterious and dangerous virus. His congregation, however, denied that there was any danger, and it was hard to reach consensus because it was never clear to him that the minister held authority. He concluded he was in the wrong church. Though he never imagined doing an online search for a church six states away and moving his family so far in a pandemic, it was the right move for them.

That feeling was confirmed when he announced his resignation. At first the church was stunned and felt betrayed. Then, they blamed him and turned resentful. Though his experience was excruciating at the time, the move was a good one, and the pandemic ended up being a blessing. Without this crisis he believes he would have stayed in a church where his leadership might never have been appreciated. He feels he is a better pastor now, one that is less invested in pleasing people and clearer about what he needs and what the church needs.

As mentioned earlier, Barna Church Research reported that 42 percent of clergy seriously considered resigning, retiring, or leaving the profession during the pandemic, a striking statistic that led religious analysts and, indeed, other professionals to dub this crisis "the Great Resignation." In his article on the subject, John Wemberly noted that the number of clergy considering quitting full-time ministry in 2022 was twice the former number (21 percent) reported in 2021. He sees this spate of resignations as a continuation of a long term trend, marked by "the five R's: retirement, relocation, reconsideration, reshuffling, and reluctance."[1] Many of those who left the profession said it was discouraging to watch attendance diminish, but others mentioned the anger they felt directed at them as polarizing debates rocked their congregations. Over time these dynamics became soul-sapping. This second reason carried a lot of weight in our conversations. We noticed a growing trend in congregations to second-guess the judgment of the clergy, to refuse to listen to their wisdom, or to balk at the changes they recommended.

An experienced clergyman of many decades, Rabbi Carl Perkins from Needham, Massachusetts, reported sending a pastoral letter to the congregation at the start of the pandemic to reassure his people. But although he knew his people well and had a reputation for his wisdom and pastoral presence, for months, he faced lay leaders who undermined him and questioned his decisions. The synagogue

1. Wimberley "Why Stay a Pastor?"

hired a consultant, who advised the congregation to respect Perkins' authority as rabbi. Perkins told us that things got better after the consultant weighed in but the problems were never fully resolved. He announced his retirement in 2022.

❈

Methodist pastor Rev. Joanne Brown of Des Moines, Washington, was working twice as hard during the pandemic but still received lots of criticism about the worship services. Parishioners compared them to services at a church across town where there was a paid communications director. The lay personnel committee second-guessed her decisions to keep the staff during the pandemic and overrode her. She had been content in her congregation and enjoyed high approval before the pandemic. Then, everything changed and she became a target of sustained criticism. That kind of acrimony is hard in normal times; during the pandemic it proved to be a deal-breaker. Feeling hurt and angry, Brown retired after a long and distinguished career.

❈

When the pandemic crisis came, Rev. Eileen Morris from Slatersville, Rhode Island, had just nursed her husband through a long decline following his ALS diagnosis. The congregation had stepped up to assist her in the last stages of his illness, but she felt depleted, lonely, and isolated from her people in 2020. To say her loneliness was made raw by her recent loss was true, but she also spoke candidly about her growing intolerance for church life on the heels of recent church debates about whether to welcome people from the LGBTQ community. Finally, she felt she was not only grieving the loss of her husband but carrying the weight of real disappointment in her people. Altogether, it was a perfect storm; she retired and moved out of state.

❈

Although the number of clergy we found who resettled or retired was significantly less than the national average, we heard many stories about people considering leaving the profession, for the first time. The topic surfaced spontaneously in fully half of our interviews. Many clergy who reported job satisfaction and even joy in parish ministry before the pandemic were now questioning whether they would stay. People who enjoyed hospital visits, loved Bible study and were fulfilled leading worship had started to question their sense of purpose and even their professional identity. Without contact with their flocks, many felt exhausted and lost. Everything that had energized them was long gone.

No one took these decisions lightly, but the crisis offered the opportunity for a new level of honest self-appraisal. Plus, as we have reported, the crisis exposed some of the hard edges of church decision-making with targeted criticism, rough debates, and lack of trust. After months of leading their congregations alone and unhindered, as the crisis subsided many clergy faced new power struggles. Lay leaders wanted to re-exert their influence or restore some authority they felt they had lost. Some lay leaders were oblivious about safety protocols, and undeterred in their determination to "get back to normal," whatever that meant to them. These congregations now resisted the clergy's leadership, sometimes in ugly ways.

Ironically, it was that period at the end of the crisis when some clergy experienced heightened frustration, sleepless nights, and new levels of disillusionment that made their jobs untenable. Rev. Amy Lignitz Harken from Mattapoisett, Massachusetts, described her experience: "It was like all the ugliness was frozen for about eighteen months. Then, despite any former accolades and sincere expressions of appreciation I received, when things started to "thaw," the ugliness was still there and in some cases worse, as though the demons were making up for lost time."

In his article "Why Stay a Pastor?" John Wimberly encourages ecclesiastical denominations to consider making recruitment, training, and life-long support of clergy leaders their top priority.[2] We agree that clergy need many more resources from professionals trained in vocational discernment and congregational systems theory. But they also need places where they can get coaching from

2. Wimberly, "Why Stay a Pastor?"

experienced senior mentors without fearing there will be penalties for being honest about their concerns or doubts. They need places where they can ask hard questions about leadership issues and feel heard knowing that they are not alone in asking these questions.

Barna Research reported in November 2021 that 46 percent of pastors under forty-five were considering quitting full-time ministry. Of those considering quitting, 51 percent served mainline Protestant denominations. This is sobering news for mainline organized religion.[3] On every criteria of well-being—spiritual, physical, emotional, vocational, and financial—two-thirds of the respondents in the Barna Research poll of nine hundred Protestant senior pastors reported that they were struggling. These findings span all ages of clergy and every level of leadership, but continue to be at crisis levels for younger clergy. Factors such as loneliness, debt, lack of support, and general dissatisfaction have long been identified as factors in clergy dissatisfaction, especially in people new to the profession.

Programs like the Bethany Fellows, developed in 1999 to address this pattern, have prioritized a series of retreats and year-round mentoring from seasoned pastors in several Protestant denominations. According to Rev. Kim Gage Ryan, Bethany Fellows director, the program is making a difference. There are early signs that it has reversed some of the disturbing trends and demonstrated how support, in the key first five years in the profession, can give pastors a cohort, and a sense of connection. The hope is that individuals in programs like this will find people to consult with in times of confusion so they stay engaged in ministry. As many as 90 percent of the participants in the Bethany Fellows continue to remain in parish ministry, a striking statistic.[4]

---

3. "38% of US Pastors."

4. We want to thank David Shirey, who has served as a mentor in the Bethany Fellows Program for bringing this organization to our attention, and Kim Gage Ryan for her time in explaining her work, as well as her support of our work.

ISOLATION

Clergy expressed to us that they felt abandoned in a time of great need. Not only were they on the firing line in their churches, many could not find resources from their denominations or judicatories. While they appreciated the guidance they received initially when it was time to close their buildings in March 2020 after that many failed to feel supported. Those who belonged to a clergy support group, or who heard from their bishops or district superintendents felt as though someone understood their struggles and saw their efforts. Those who did not hear from the judicatories were disappointed and felt invisible. When advice came it was often described as being out of touch or irrelevant, which added insult to injury and heightened the clergy's sense of isolation from the very bodies that had ordained them to service, and to which they felt loyal.

Across all the interviews, with few exceptions, clergy reported disappointment with their denominational leaders. As we tried to understand this complaint we recognized that clergy had felt especially disappointed because they were hurt. You can only feel hurt like that when you believe in your judicatory—and rely on it. The consistent complaint we heard was that conference staff, synod leaders, presbyters, and bishops did not reach out or that their support was often too little or too late. To be fair, the people running most denominations are clergy themselves, and they were also operating without a playbook. However, the clergy we spoke to said that they had to lead worship weekly, fully prepared or not. They did not have the luxury of waiting for their denominational leaders to get their bearings.

Clergy loyalty and gratitude was genuine and heartfelt when a district superintendent or presbytery leader kept in personal touch with a pastor. In Montana, for example, Rev. Laura Folkwein reported that her conference executives set up her peer support group and she was grateful. In several states we heard similar stories about colleague groups that worked, but they were scattered examples and not the norm.

Clergy found that Facebook forums became the place to ask questions and share advice, and many were loyal to friends far away. These peer-led cohorts became the place to get answers for everything from technology to liturgy to leadership issues. It was these young clergy groups, clergy moms, clergy dads, women clergy, and large steeple groups that became trusted advisors for one another.

Whether they reached out to colleagues for help or became more vulnerable with their own people, clergy learned to lead differently in many cases. They could see new strengths in themselves because COVID had helped them find new ways to lead. Rev. Nancy Rosas from Buffalo, New York, thinks the pandemic made her "more human" and relatable. Now, she "shares her vulnerability and fears more easily." As a consequence her people feel closer, and so she is less alone, a "more collaborative leader."

NEW DATA

As recently as July 2023 new research from the Barna Group reported on dangerous levels of loneliness among the clergy they polled. Barna compared data from 2015 with a more recent study in 2022 and found that loneliness had increased significantly over these seven years. In 2015, 42 percent of clergy reported loneliness, but by 2022 fully 65 percent reported feelings of being alone and isolated. When the Barna Group analyzed what had changed they discovered that feelings of support had decreased significantly over this time. The big difference was that in 2015, 68 percent reported feeling well supported, but by 2022 that number had dropped to 49 percent.[5] Overall the research points to a significant rise in the number of clergy who felt they were on the brink of burnout.

5. "2 Year Trends."

RECKONING

The COVID pandemic crisis sparked a deep soul search for many clergy. With only a few exceptions, everyone we interviewed asked some version of the question, "Am I called to do this?" One young pastor said, "I know I was called to show up when people are sick. I know I am called to make sense of Scripture. Those values hold true. But the pandemic has made me question everything else about my call, and I wonder whether I am doing the right thing with my life. Because of the pandemic, I even question the church's mission." There was a profound sense of disillusionment that ran through these interviews, even among those who found benefits to the ways the pandemic had stretched them. One person who "grew in the pandemic" because it made her more flexible in some ways also admitted she was thinking more about when to retire and whether to be involved in a church at all after she's retired. While all the people we spoke to have a deep and abiding commitment to faith and service—a commitment that was tried, tested, and proven in this experience, they often questioned their commitment to faith leadership in the future and wondered if they were being called to something else.

We were humbled to hear people share some of their most vulnerable concerns, often giving voice for the first time to feelings they were just beginning to recognize or articulate to themselves. The additional privilege of hearing these stories and being able to share them was not lost on us as we know well that religious leaders often maintain a very public persona and don't share personal things easily. What became clear in conversation after conversation was that the former balance most professional clergy maintain of caring for others and for themselves was thrown off in the pandemic. As the needs of the parish, the community, and the world became overwhelming, it was easy for ministers to lose themselves in the collective trauma. So, as caretakers of others, it was even harder for clergy to admit during the pandemic crisis how wounded they themselves had become.

The health and vitality of religious life relies on its leaders. Without their enthusiasm, things are precarious as religious institutions face an uncertain future. Studies continue to show that organized religion is declining in the US, a trend that started before the pandemic but was exacerbated by the crisis.[6] Now those concerns carry new gravitas. Rev. Scott Spencer in Cranston, Rhode Island, rarely thought before the pandemic that the purpose of his work was to ensure the survival of his church. Now it was often on his mind. Given his success growing his congregation, raising funds, reaching new people, and running a widely known prison ministry, his lament about how the pandemic stripped him of so much that fed his soul is sobering.

A SENSE OF PRIDE

Even bearing these concerns in mind, the clergy were also legitimately proud to have come through the pandemic, having kept their people together and having led congregations that remained solvent financially. We heard that pride growing in their voices as they recounted all they had done and how much adversity they'd had to face to do it. Many clergy also acknowledged that they had grown. They were genuinely pleased by their own ingenuity, the times they trusted their instincts, and the ways their prayers were answered often in unexpected or whimsical ways. Many had avoided the temptation to obsess about mistakes and could laugh at early efforts to improvise. They forgave themselves for being imperfect. They remembered that their spirits were buoyed by new ideas. They recounted new inventions, conceived out of necessity but now part of their congregation's lexicon: online fundraisers, "Anytime Church," podcasts, faith hikes, hybrid meetings, online worship, and sermons featuring video illustrations. Pushed to do new things, they became more spontaneous preachers, more courageous innovators, and more prophetic speakers.

---

6. Christians continue to make up the majority in the US and participation is twelve points lower in 2021 than it was in 2011 according to Pew Research (Pew Research Center, "Americans Growing Less Religious").

7

What Does This Mean for the Future?

We've tried hard not to lose who we are, but we're not sure who we'll be. I wonder if the new wine can fit into the wineskins of our churches.
—Rev. Randy Bush, Pittsburgh, Pennsylvania

"The stained glass of the future is the video screen. Now we have new windows through which we can look to hear the story of faith"
—Rev. Patrick Wrisley, Fort Lauderdale, Florida

"I'm not sure how to answer your questions; talk to me in five years."
—Fr. Greg Christakos, Marlborough, Massachusetts

"I always thought of myself as an optimist. I understood that the church is not quick to change, but now I wonder about the future"
—Rev. Jeremy Lopez, Tonawanda, New York

The Perpetual Pivot

Rev. Hollie Woodruff of Richmond, Virginia, told her congregation that they could not go back to the way things were before the pandemic: "Too much has changed, and we've changed." As a new pastor she discovered that many people felt the communion table was far away from where they sat for services. So during the pandemic she worked with the worship committee to remove eight rows of pews and move the communion table to the center of the sanctuary floor. That change had a profound effect, much more far-reaching than a simple rearrangement of furniture. It carried the weight of a symbolic shift with dramatic ripple effects for her congregation. With the communion table in the center of the worshiping community, older parishioners felt included and younger ones felt invited to full participation. The change transformed how the congregation related to one another and how they related to the sacred elements of worship. At Woodruff's church, the pandemic laid the groundwork for thinking about the worship space differently and set the stage for this transformation.

❦

Pandemics are never isolated incidents. People experience them in a unique historical context, but they have lasting impacts. They change the landscape of our lives, leaving many families grieving and many institutions tossed into the winds of change. They leave a lot of devastation in their wake, and with those losses come huge shifts in culture. Major health crises like the one we have just experienced, and are continuing to live through, produce rippling effects for years and even decades. We predict that historians will be examining this pandemic as a hinge moment in history, a time when everything changed. They will evaluate trends from before the pandemic and compare them to trends after the crisis.

Indeed, in the fourteenth century when an illness known as the Black Death ravaged Europe and the Middle East, the Arab historian Ibu Khaldun wrote, "Civilization both in the East and West was visited by a destructive plague which devastated nations

What Does This Mean for the Future?

and caused populations to vanish."[1] He described horrific city landscapes, marked by piles of dead bodies. The horror from that pandemic was re-lived in scenes from New York City at the worst of the COVID pandemic. But that's not the only parallel.

Historians from the 1300s also describe a different and utterly unnatural set of scenes in the countryside, where ripened fields went unharvested, fruit and vegetables dropped to the ground to rot because the villages were hollowed out by disease, and no one was left to bring in the harvest. The experience was so harrowing that it sparked a world-wide reassessment of what gave life purpose. The survivors of the Black Death were so shaken by their own proximity to death that they became acutely aware of the gift of life. So, they asked new questions about their lives and insisted on new answers.

For example, many serfs in England were no longer willing to endure former hardships and began to demand higher wages. Prices in the mid 1300's rose twenty-seven percent and workers threatened to leave the fields and seek other employment if wages did not keep up with inflation. The labor movement was born in the Middle Ages, in response to the Black Plague.

Writing for the New York Times, MT Anderson said the tensions, labor laws, reprisals and torture of workers fleeing serfdom marked the start of a societal upheaval, all sparked by the Black Plague. "On one side a newly emboldened workforce demanded a living wage, a chance to flourish; on the other kings and councils, lords and wealthy commoners were determined that nothing change."[2] Eventually things exploded as riots broke out in the middle and end of the 1300s. Peasants leveled houses, burned records, and killed the nobility. In reprisal, the gentry started to burn villages and slaughter the inhabitants. Violent class warfare spread across Europe and England and, as time went on, mobs grew so angry that they also targeted Jews and immigrants, who they believed threatened their jobs. The sense of futility that had been growing over time blossomed in the wake of the plague and

1. Anderson, "After a Plague."
2. Anderson, "After a Plague."

affected not only peasants but also tradespeople, merchants, and clergy. Plagues often foment such fundamental unrest, and people cannot help but question everything, so that nothing is ever quite the same afterward.

In similar ways today, modern workers from all walks of life are reevaluating their career options, what they are willing to do for a living, and how much they need to earn to make it worth their time, talent, and energy to support themselves and their families. After months of working remotely, many office workers fail to see the need to be in an office environment to do their jobs and have come to prefer working remotely, at least part-time. While our labor movement has not endured such a massive transformation as the one in the fourteenth century, we see similar patterns at work in the world today. More and more people are questioning the meaning of their jobs and how they want to spend their day. Similar forces have sparked the clergy reckoning we examined in the last chapter.

It would be premature to assume that we have finished with the COVID-19 virus. There is every reason to believe that we will be facing wave after wave of COVID variants in the years ahead. So, it is too early to know what the future holds. However, it was clear to us as we spoke to clergy from across the country that the pandemic raised many questions about their needs and aspirations but also about the direction of our religious institutions—the synagogues and churches[3]—that shape religious life in this country. When the pandemic began in 2020 religion was already in a time of transition. Mainline Protestant denominations were reporting record losses of members, and many congregations were already in steep decline. But as clergy lived through the pandemic, even with its expanding online audiences, they began to question how this public health crisis would reshape their work and the institutions that they served.

---

3. This may be true for mosques and other houses of worship but it would be speculation on our part, because that is beyond the scope of our inquiry. Admittedly, it is stretch to make many assumptions about synagogues based on one interview.

What Does This Mean for the Future?

In Susan Beaumont's book, *How to Lead When You Don't Know Where You're Going,* she provides a framework for approaching times of crisis. Beaumont identified this period in church history as a liminal time, a time of change and transformation. Her words were prescient coming as they did even before 2020.[4] The pandemic prompted people to reevaluate past practices and reinvent new ones in church and society, offering a prime example of a liminal chapter in history. Beaumont warns against the temptation to rush during liminal times, as disorientation is to be expected. While it may be tempting to rely on old leadership patterns characterized by setting goals, making plans, and organizing new projects, these patterns of leadership, formerly so successful, may not ultimately provide the best path forward. Instead, she counsels that clergy operate from a mindset of experimentation and wonder, questioning what the next chapter will look like in our communities of faith. Her advice supported the instinct we found in many faith leaders of relying more on spiritual practices to support and heighten their discernment skills in this time of change.

Phyllis Tickle provides another helpful lens for this time period.[5] In her comprehensive analysis of the broad span of church history she identifies a pattern of significant change every five hundred years, especially in the Judeo-Christian tradition. With some regularity, every five centuries major shifts occur in organized religious practice and self understanding dating back to 1000 BCE, with the last such transition in the sixteenth century when Europe was convulsed in a religious upheaval known as the Protestant Reformation. Tickle says that faith communities are currently in another such time of transformation, right on schedule. If Tickle's thesis is correct, and her evidence is convincing, the Christian Church has been in the throes of this transition for over one hundred years, a transition she identifies as the Great Emergence.

---

4. The term "liminal" means occupying a position at or on both sides of a boundary, often in a stage of transition. For example, anthropologists in the nineteenth century identified initiation rites as times when people experienced a liminal space, as they completed childhood but prior to adulthood.

5. Tickle, *Great Emergence.*

The Perpetual Pivot

Every transformation is characterized by cultural change as well as technological developments that combine to challenge religious norms. Certainly the upheaval in Europe during the last such religious reinvention was heralded by the invention of the printing press, movable type, and new ink, all of which changed communication in the same radical ways that the invention of the internet has in our own time. But the religious transformation of the sixteenth century was also characterized by fierce disputes about doctrine and violent reprisals including burning heretics at the stake. The violence of these punishments for "heresy" point to the seriousness of the threat experienced by leaders determined to curb the dramatic shifts in religious tradition. Such is the sense of desperation which accompanies religious deconstruction. While these changes may usher in a new era, eventually, it is a process of many decades and takes time before that newness can be embraced. Initially, the immediate experience is one of profound loss.

Many clergy mentioned the work of Beaumont and Tickle. That points to an appreciation for the fact that we are living in a time of shifting religious templates. It is as though the very ground is breaking up beneath the clergy's feet. Faith leaders who have often been the symbols of certainty in changing times feel less and less certain about what the future will look like, or how to lead others in spiritual practice. Many of these comments also came with a sense of wonder as they watch the forces of change at work all around, forces that are bigger than all of us.

PERMANENT CHANGES

Rev. Brad Berqfalk of Arvada, Colorado, said this experience had changed not only what he does in his work but what he values. He takes the requirements of ministry more lightly. Where formerly it would have been unheard of to offer the sacraments at home, now he encourages his online audience to serve themselves wherever they are watching. The pandemic has also made him more flexible about how he leads his classes and evaluates worship attendance. "The conditions that caused these changes were not ideal, but the response

What Does This Mean for the Future?

to this crisis has made me more flexible and more resilient. There is a great sorting going on now for churches. With worship online people have the opportunity to visit big churches with well-known preachers. They can choose to organize their religious life in brand new ways."

❀

These changes in religious life, once unimaginable, are now permanent, according to our respondents. Internet worship, Zoom meetings, and hybrid classes are the standard in many congregations. So also is the flexibility of the worshiping public to try a variety of services all while keeping in loose contact with several at once, and expressing loyalty to all these places of worship in the same way that people feel loyal to a favorite correspondent or television personality.

Rev. Ruth Snyder, of Tonawanda, New York, is rethinking everything. She is working to keep her online audience for worship and often reminds people that their Christmas Eve Service was viewed by someone in Paris. She stumbled onto a successful venue for her summer Vacation Bible School when she held it on the lawn as she attracted a much larger group of community kids, and town-wide attention. So, that change is here to stay. She continues to try to learn the lessons of the pandemic and re-envision church life through the lens of this experience.

❀

Like many clergy, Rev. Candi Ashenden of Athol, Massachusetts, discovered that the online worship experience completely changed how she leads worship, especially how she preaches. These days she creates every sermon with the visual impact at the front of her mind. "I begin my sermon preparation by imagining how to bring the message to life with images, pictures, and video. Now, everything I do is much more visual, from the children's message to the liturgy and the sermon. That means using pictures, graphic images, and film. I view the entire message of the morning first as a visual message, and *the words, while important, are not the driving force. This pandemic completely transformed the way I see communications as central to the church's work, so that now I have plans to add a communications staff person to my team, so I can include film in worship, and throughout parish life."*

❖

In similar ways Rev. Mary Bauer from Appleton, Wisconsin, reports her eyes were opened to how much ministry can be done on Zoom. She has led her congregation to create baptism workshops on Zoom to fit the busy schedules of young couples. Her church created wedding workshops on Zoom so couples can participate from a distance as they plan their wedding in Wisconsin. She has designed a strategic vision process using Zoom and runs staff meetings online. "In a demanding and mobile world this kind of telecommunication tool allows us to include staff with jobs in the Twin Cities (a five-hour drive) as well as busy parishioners on the move."

LEADERSHIP INNOVATIONS

Many clergy assumed more authority in the pandemic and grew more accustomed to making decisions. The churches that accepted this new arrangement as a positive improvement were successful in keeping their pastors; those that rebelled or struggled to compete with their clergy for leadership often found their clergy were no longer willing to remain. Something about this crisis reminded faith leaders of their essential role and value. When the worth of their work was not respected, they questioned what they were doing in their congregation, or in this profession. Many, like the serfs in the fourteenth century, found their voices and refused to stay in places where their leadership was not valued. "Therefore, more congregations are coming out of the pandemic without leadership because they cannot find a replacement as the overall number of clergy declines." The labor shortage within the clergy, which parallels shortages in other industries, is reshaping worship in some parts of the country as more congregations search for ways to operate without a pastor, reports the Wall Street Journal.[6] When clergy remained in their congregations, they changed their leadership patterns, becoming some combination of what Rhode Island pastor Rev. Scott Spencer described as a "benevolent dictator and good listener." Even if clergy tempered this stronger approach with kindness and respect, it has been a new role nonetheless.

❧

"It was clear that we were religious leaders during this pandemic," said Fr. Greg Christakos. "Sometimes when church life is busy, I go through life on cruise control. I get through because I stumble through. In this pandemic people saw us as leaders. We were leaders because we had to be. People will look to us for leadership in different ways going forward. There was no precedent for this, but what we did during the pandemic created a blueprint for the future, a blueprint that folks will consult long after this is over."

Everyone we spoke to said that this pandemic has permanently changed their congregations, and not all the changes were bad. But they all require adjustment and further evaluation.

WORSHIP—HOW DO WE PRAISE GOD NOW?

Many clergy believe the pandemic accelerated the need for technology in worship, and now, as we look to the future, the congregations that are technologically savvy will seize the moment and use technology in ways we have not yet imagined. This transition will be a bigger one than just streaming our services. It will challenge faith communities to consider who their audience is each week.

The question of how to combine the online and in-person congregations looms large for many congregations going forward. Many churches have continued to have a robust online audience from their elderly members, people whose mobility may be challenged but who also possess newfound computer skills following

---

6. Lovett, "Houses of Worship."

the pandemic. Some churches installed huge screens in the sanctuary to create a hybrid worship experience where viewers at home can see and be seen, a visual connection between people at home and those in the pews. Once in-person worship resumed regularly, many churches increased their staff and added equipment to aid in live-streaming their worship services on platforms like YouTube, Facebook, or the church's website.

But there may be a problem in this "solution." Keeping the online audience by livestreaming an in-person service ignores all the lessons learned in the pandemic about how to attract new people to online worship. The most effective way to find new viewers and ensure that they would return was to create worship aimed at the online audience—services intended to be no longer than twenty-four minutes. Typical online worship services that are livestreamed run well over an hour, often beginning with footage of folks milling around or holding inaudible conversations. Long services with a slow start and ten minutes of local announcements hold minimal appeal for online worshipers. It may be possible to retain an audience that enjoys a strong connection to the congregation, but any effort to attract new members online will require a more intentional approach.

In the future clergy need to consider how online worship might be used to market the message of faith. Congregations that hope to keep attracting new people online, as they did in the pandemic, will need to have these longer services edited to a more suitable length to appeal to online viewers. That will mean eliminating some parts and emphasizing others. Designing online worship is a different enterprise, and faith leaders need to ask what components are essential in a shorter experience. The pandemic taught us that photos or video combine well with musical sequences. Producing effective online worship will require that they be recorded, edited, and produced with good quality sound, robotic cameras that allow several angles, teleprompters, and a polished product that compares more favorably with televised productions.

The online worship service also attracts people seeking a faith community. Watching online is often the first step in a process of

WHAT DOES THIS MEAN FOR THE FUTURE?

research, like scoping out real estate online before you take the house tour. Clergy should plan an experience that showcases their best features, to appeal to online viewers who are evaluating the music, the message, and the overall vibe of the congregation as they assess whether the church is the right fit for them. As we enter a new age of technology it will be increasingly important to prioritize budgets for technology staff. Rev. Fritz Fowler from Lansdale, Pennsylvania, recognized that a technology budget in the church of the future will be as important as the music budget in churches of the past, especially for congregations that hope to grow.

MEMBERSHIP—WHO ARE WE?

For many years the size of a congregation was used as the prime indicator of its strength as a spiritual community. However there have never been standard metrics for compiling these statistics. Some congregations count families; others count adults; some count people in a geographic area who identify as part of the parish. To make matters more complex, the count is often subjective, especially when clergy themselves hope to keep their numbers high. However, the pandemic raised these census issues to a new level as taking attendance at worship raised so many new questions. Were those who found the congregation online in the pandemic potential new "members" or perpetual "visitors"? Does membership depend on in-person participation? Should membership assume a financial component? Should online participants be afforded the rights to participate in congregational decision-making such as voting on important issues? If congregations seek to integrate the online congregation into the in-person congregation how many services should someone attend before a pastor reaches out? Should the online audience be invited to an orientation class or a fellowship group or a decision-making meeting? Should they receive the sacraments? Are they eligible to become lay leaders?

Traditional membership expectations included in-person worship, completion of a class, a commitment to attend worship regularly, and financial contributions. During the pandemic these criteria changed. Some congregations considered two tiers of membership—in-person and online. A few churches admitted people to full membership who had only participated online and never darkened the door. Our conversations brought larger questions to mind. Is online worship aimed at members of the congregation who were too sick or afraid to attend in person? Is it meant to attract a whole new audience of people seeking a virtual community of faith? Does it offer an attractive portal for church-shoppers? What is the nature of church membership in a time of technological change?

Given all the concerns we heard about church membership during the pandemic, we assumed that many congregations would rely on databases in this crisis. But such was not the case. While databases might provide the kind of information that would have helped to alleviate the feelings that haunted faith leaders, the feelings that they were losing people, few used them in the crisis. While they could track participation across the demographics of the congregation, track shifts in participation, or even run scenarios, very few clergy relied on them. In our sample Rev. Dawn Adams, from Brimfield, Massachusetts, was the biggest advocate for using a database. She found it helpful to maintain statistics on her people—where they were, how they participated, how often they got a visit, or how much they contributed.

Even those clergy with well-oiled programs for attracting and integrating new members had systems based on in-person connections. Robbed of these personal interactions, the engine for their church vitality was all but abandoned. In his four-thousand-member church in Nebraska, Rev. Jim Keck explained that they needed to add two hundred members every year just to stay even, given the attrition rates due to transfers, and deaths. In 2020, the church added one hundred new members, and in 2021 it added one hundred and fifty. So, in Keck's view, the church began 2022 behind by 150 people. While these are large numbers, every congregation had similar challenges proportional to their size.

These membership concerns all point to a larger question. Does the concept of church membership need to be redefined?

What Does This Mean for the Future?

Some clergy wondered whether it matters at all. In the past, weekly worship was the gold standard, and a primary metric for church "success," but recent data shows that of the people who belong to a congregation, weekly worship is declining and has become more rare. According to Gallup, 34 percent of Americans attended worship once or twice a month in 2019, with an average of 1.7 times a month. That percentage decreased to 31 percent in 2020 and 28 percent in 2021.[7] Of the 360,000 churches in the United States, attendance declined so significantly during the pandemic that by December 2022, only 50–65 percent of members had returned to in-person worship.[8] If this decline marks a true trend, that is a serious decline with far-reaching implications for the future. Many clergy referred to this data with a sense of apprehension.

RECAPTURING THE AUDIENCE OF YOUNG FAMILIES AS WELL AS SERVING AN AGING POPULATION

Many clergy also reported that the ministry to children was the biggest loss for churches during the pandemic. It remains the most concerning trend for many faith leaders as families with children have been the slowest to return. In mainline churches, worship for young families was almost exclusively online or outdoors as parents were understandably protective of their kids. The longest delay for vaccines was those for young children. As drug manufacturers were understandably cautious about children's medications, it took twenty-seven months for young children to have the option to be vaccinated. Even after school resumed in-person and many children started to attend classes without vaccines, church parents were hesitant to expose their children to another group of people in their faith community, seeing it as an unnecessary risk. In some cases, families with children avoided entering the church building for two years, which is a very long hiatus in the life of children.

7. Jones, "US Church Attendance."
8. "Attendance at Religious Services."

The Perpetual Pivot

Even before the pandemic, many religious educators were questioning the old models of Sunday school education. It was hard to ignore the competition for family time on Sundays as sports programs expanded throughout the weekend hours. Some religious educators had already been experimenting with evening programs, family retreats, and take-home lessons for children and youth. During the pandemic, with a dearth of options for families inside their buildings, many congregations from Vermont to Alaska turned to outdoor programming. That trend of planning outdoor activities seems to be here to stay as it was widely successful. Short-term curriculum delivered to a family's doorstep was also popular during liturgical seasons such as Advent or Lent; some congregations expanded this approach and used it throughout the program year.

However, two years is a very long time to be out of the habit of attending religious programs in-person and it remains to be seen which percentage of families who had formerly been active in religious institutions, simply lost interest in organized religion altogether. This is not an insignificant loss. While reliable data is hard to find, reports of congregations losing almost half of their families were not uncommon. The concern here, of course, is that youth and families are a crucial demographic for congregational vitality and growth as they represent the future of religious institutions. It's also quite possible that this former metric of vitality in religious communities—the presence of a robust children's program—is also being called into question. As we make the case for the fact that the future is uncertain, perhaps the very metrics for vitality are also in flux.

Rev. Jeremy Lopez from Tonawanda, New York, said the pandemic has changed organized religion so fundamentally that it will be impossible for churches to ever regain some of their former strength. He is troubled by the concern that families who have been worshiping online will not return to the pew. His best estimate was that one third will never come back to the church, one third will come back immediately and stay connected, and one third will remain on the fence. He worries that the church has not done all it

What Does This Mean for the Future?

can to retain families with children, and they simply will not return. How much energy will it take, if it is even possible, to rebuild these congregations? The task is daunting when as many as 50 percent of some congregations have proved that they can go for months and months without being connected in person to their congregation or to their pastor.

We are still learning the lessons of the pandemic. However the most recent data illustrates some surprising trends. The Hartford Institute for Religion Research at Hartford International University for Religion and Peace (formerly Hartford Seminary) released a report in August 2023. While it contains a mix of messages about congregational recovery, several conclusions belie the fears of many clergy in our survey. Here are some of their discoveries:

1. Religious communities remain unsettled and still in flux. Churches have not arrived at a place of stasis and normalcy, no matter what members wish for.

2. Attendance continues to rebound. Not only has the in-person worshiping congregation rebounded, but when it is counted along with the virtual congregation, the total number of worshipers is up by 15 percent over pre-pandemic statistics.

3. Church finances are also increased with median giving up 25 percent when adjusted for inflation, a "remarkable increase." As suspected, these surveys found that the more churches emphasized online and electronic giving, the greater per capita giving rose.

4. Volunteer participation has risen to 35 percent, almost at pre-pandemic levels of 40 percent.

5. Finally, perhaps the biggest surprise in this new data is that conflict levels have decreased between 5 and 25 percent. While it seems counterintuitive in a nation where public debate can become acrimonious, the Hartford study suggests that the "result might be that the last three years have created congregations with attenders that are more homogeneous."[9] Another possibility is that

---

9. See "Back to Normal?" One caveat about this conclusion is that there are several ways to look at the data, depending on how you analyze attendance changes. So while it is encouraging, it is not entirely conclusive, and numbers are very much in flux.

the pandemic had a sobering effect on some people, an effect that made them more likely to choose their battles.

As congregations look to the future, it seems likely that some will continue to rebound. In these and all congregations one of the challenges will be to serve two demographics with very different needs—young families and senior members. Indeed, faith communities remain one of the few places that are attempting to bring such a broad spectrum of the population into close community settings.

One lesson from this crisis was that the seniors proved to be resilient and committed to their congregations in the crisis. For example, a number of clergy in our survey mentioned their surprise at the way seniors citizens improved their computer skills in order to stay connected. In a population whose technology skills had been discounted, they faced the technological challenges head-on. However, many clergy also echoed the concerns of Rev. Jeremy Lopez, asking, "If congregations fail to attract younger families what does that trend portend for the future?" Behind their question is another one: "Is it even possible to attract such a wide spread of ages to the same set of programs or worship services?" Does one-size-church programming fit all our demographic constituents? Furthermore, are congregations chasing the younger demographic with programs that don't interest them and underestimating the seniors who remain determined to stay involved?

HOW DO WE SUPPORT CONGREGATIONS IN THE FUTURE?

Many clergy voiced surprise at the generosity of their people and of the general public in the crisis. What they discovered is that people were generous when they were spiritually nurtured, when they felt needed, and when they caught the vision of their faith leaders. That is not new, but the pandemic reminded people of this truth. Despite all the changes in worship and money collection, most clergy reported, often with wonder in their voices, that their congregations did not default on their financial obligations. They

What Does This Mean for the Future?

may have lost rental income during the pandemic, but they saved in other ways with fewer expenses. Their budgets were balanced with impressive levels of generosity during the pandemic and record giving in some cases.

This seemed counter-intuitive but we believe there are lessons to be learned in this trend. Without social events, classes for kids, pastoral visits or adult education, some clergy failed to understand why people remained so invested. During COVID they were actually getting less for their money. Why were they so generous? One answer is that they did not view their gifts as payment for services. Instead, they gave generously as a way to stay connected to their faith community, to their friends, and even to total strangers. They also sent contributions as a way to encourage their faith leaders. They sent gifts to show gratitude for a moving sermon or a vespers podcast. They gave in response to words of sorely needed hope.

Though clergy might have questioned the monetary value of what people were receiving in the pandemic, and several people mentioned this in these interviews, the congregations in these churches showed no signs of seeing church life in such transactional terms. While clergy may be well aware of the administrative costs of running a parish, most members don't think in terms of paying for education or social engagement. What the pandemic demonstrated was that the generosity in many congregations was never tied to the tangible benefits they received. Instead, it was tied to the way people felt encouraged or inspired. There is no price tag for that kind of gratitude, and folks responded generously because they'd been touched or encouraged to persevere and because they felt part of something bigger than themselves. Though it was rare to include online audiences in congregational life or to ask them for donations, it may become a tool in the future. Online audiences that felt needed or included proved to be very generous too.

❧

We saw that at Susan's church on Cape Cod, when we needed to upgrade our equipment for online worship. When we decided to raise funds for a new camera, lighting, soundboard, software, and computer, we appealed to the online congregation as well as the church members. We asked our online audience to join established members in considering sending gifts to improve the worship services they were enjoying. To our surprise, the response exceeded our expectations. While that fundraising was primarily supported by current members of the congregation, several people whose only connection to the church was virtual worship sent contributions. In some cases they also began to send regular monthly donations even after the appeal for technology funds was successful.

❖

Another example of community fund-raising happened in Rev. Nico Reijn's church in Girdwood, Alaska, when non-church members contributed generously to the community center he was starting on church property. They gave volunteer hours but also monetary gifts to support the venture. Across the country when churches organized food and clothing drives many people outside the church felt inspired to contribute with cash, in kind gifts and volunteer hours.

On Cape Cod, at the height of the pandemic shut-down, Peggy organized four successful community-wide book sales on the lawn of the church. Coordinating with public health officials, she organized these events using tables set up to encourage safe browsing. The response to these events was overwhelming as people reported they had not bought books in many months and were eager for new titles. After the first book sale many customers returned to donate their own books and puzzles, highly sought items in the pandemic. Those donations made each successive sale possible. The lawn book sales positioned the church as a place that understood what people needed and provided considerable revenue, with profit from the four sales being $10,000. (That is thousands of books, at $.50 each). Others made outright contributions in gratitude for the event. Beyond the monetary success of these sales was the sense that it provided a way for community members to feel a part of something. By donating to future sales they helped us but also were helped to feel needed and valuable.

WHAT DOES THIS MEAN FOR THE FUTURE?

We mentioned this example and the other ones around the country because they point to a blurring of the line between members and non-members that happens when churches take the lead on addressing community needs. Increasingly, this may be a model for church leaders to consider going forward.

REAL ESTATE LESSONS—WHAT DID THE PANDEMIC TEACH US ABOUT OUR BUILDINGS?

Online and hybrid meetings are another innovation that has come to stay. This option adds a new level of convenience for groups doing congregational business, attending classes, or joining a small group. Zoom and similar platforms have revolutionized this aspect of church life. But they have also eliminated the need for many meetings inside religious buildings. This raises the question about whether churches need all of their real estate in the future. How do faith communities justify owning so many empty meeting rooms? Even as churches revive in-person programs, many churches have not been fully restored to former levels of activity. Clergy are asking if there is a better use for these rooms that are only partially utilized. This question prompts another question: Is this an opportunity to re-imagine church buildings and expand the congregation's influence in the community though mixed-used space? Just as many businesses have been reimagining how to use empty office space, faith leaders are asking similar questions about their real estate. Pioneers like Revs. Loletta Barrett, Elizabeth Goodman, and Nico Reijns began to reimagine their buildings as community space, and plenty of other pastors are considering similar options.

"Before the pandemic, I saw how buildings weighed down our congregations," said Rev. Quentin Chin from Southampton, Massachusetts. "Ownership costs inordinately consumed resources, both financial and human energy. Responsibility for real estate stymied long-term planning because people were constantly worried about annual bills and the need to raise money year-round. Then we spent a year and a half not worshiping in our buildings and survived. So I wonder, is our current building truly necessary or can churches *reduce the space they use in their buildings and find a way to monetize what can be described as extra space?* I believe that churches should work over the next few years to reimagine their relationship with their facilities so they can share the total ownership costs with another organization or shed the total ownership costs completely."

The final lesson, which only a few clergy raised, but which may become a salient one, is how to make religious spaces safer in a future where we might have to prepare for more contagious viruses and a string of COVID variants. In the aftermath of this pandemic, as faith leaders endeavor to return to normal, it may be a hard sell to try to evaluate air quality, upgrade filters, or improve HVAC systems to be prepared for the next public health challenge. One of the lessons of this pandemic might well be that faith communities should ensure that they have plans in place for another virus, or even a bad flu season. If religious communities rely on the shared experience of encouraging people to crowd into sacred spaces, then faith leaders should be committed to making those very spaces as safe as possible, now and in the future.

NO TURNING BACK FROM THIS UNEXPECTED RENAISSANCE

The COVID 19 pandemic ushered in an unexpected renaissance in many congregations with creative transformations of worship, leadership and programs. Most clergy agreed that they cannot go back to the way they were before the pandemic. But questions loom large. With awe and confusion, Rev. Eileen Morris from Slatersville, Rhode Island, wondered, "What is the goal of the church today? It had always been to get people in, to put butts in the pews. I knew how to do that successfully. These days I'm not sure what the current goals are." This is a time of quandary but also of spiritual reawakening.

Rev. Ellen Jennings from Washington, DC, said, "We need to be open to the next reformation, which is fomented by a crisis of meaning." Perhaps religious leaders need to learn from how book groups and yoga classes inspire people. Spirituality is flowing

What Does This Mean for the Future?

through new channels and it may call for a reworking of liturgies, theologies, prayers and programs. In Wisconsin, Rev. Mary Bauer believes the pandemic influenced her "to lift up her calling as a church visionary. It has also given her permission to fail and be more spontaneous." While she does not seek change for its own sake, as a leader she embraces the job of shepherding her people through the change.

Most clergy we met through our interviews still feel the tension between the surge of creativity sparked by the crisis and the push by seasoned members to get back to all the familiar patterns of church life. That tension between people who want to push into new faith frontiers and those who long for restoring pre-pandemic patterns will continue to challenge church leaders. The fact that those memories remain enshrined in people's minds does not necessarily make them accurate. Yet the memories themselves have been associated with former successes. If it were possible to erase the thirty months of illness and upset, many people would gladly like to do so. As that is not possible, some would prefer to pretend that the pandemic never happened and try to forget it. Indeed, historians wonder if that was the case after the devastating Spanish Influenza pandemic one century ago. In 2020, public health officials looked in vain for information about that crisis in public health. The dearth of information has caused some historians to speculate that people of the time were so eager to put that crisis behind them, they plunged into the Roaring Twenties, hoping to move on as though that pandemic had never occurred.

Yet, most clergy we spoke to were not prepared to "get back to normal." So, they and their congregations have come to a crossroads, a time of evaluation, a season of soul searching, and quite possibly a modern reformation. "One day people will study us, and so our job is to be listening to the Holy Spirit. It is a time of questioning and wonder," said Rev. Ruth Snyder of Tonawanda, New York.

"I'm a huge optimist. We are all on a journey just as Jesus was," said Rev. Lauran Heidenreich, of Attica, New York. "This is just a challenging part of the journey, but God is still in charge. It's an *illusion to think we can go back. The good old days never existed as they are remembered. The 1950s church is an urban legend. When I was in Minnesota and Nebraska serving farming communities, I would ask the farmers who'd been on the land for generations what the church was like. They told me church was important, and they'd go when they could. It depended on the weather or if they had a sick animal or sick child. They hoped to get to church once or twice a month. That sounds like now! We don't need to go back to anything. The resurrected Jesus hit the road, and we are called to move ahead as he did and does. Going backwards is not an option."*

❦

In Angola, Indiana, Rev. Nicole Shaw said that the pandemic has changed her leadership style. She asks "why" a lot as she talks to people, and encourages them to ask basic questions about the nature of church. Because of the pandemic Shaw leads in a way that sets a different tone, one that encourages people to expect change. The whole experience has changed her theology and view of God. She no longer thinks of God as omniscient so much as a creator, always creating. "God has the kind of creativity that sees all perspectives at once. The way the church becomes more like God is to try to see more perspectives too. The gift of COVID is that we were forced" to expand our views. Now, "the challenge and opportunity is to continue to see more than one perspective as Christ-followers, more than church-goers."

❦

In Fort Lauderdale, Florida, Rev. Patrick Wrisley was inspired by the Chinese symbol for change, which includes the sign for chaos as well as creativity. He saw a "unique swirliness of the Holy Spirit at work in churches. Reformed churches are supposed to be unafraid of change and blend the best of yesterday and today." Channeling energy from his church planter days, he came through this pandemic by letting go of the feeling that the church was resting on his shoulders and felt freed to take more risks. He embraced this time of experimentation

What Does This Mean for the Future?

without fear of failure. "This is God's project," he said. "Either we create new ways to do church, or we will die. So, we need to move beyond where we have been. If you are a creative person or institution and don't allow something creative in you to be born, then it is stillborn."

❦

Seeing this crisis as the beginning of another chapter of church history, Rev. Jim Keck, from Lincoln, Nebraska, hoped the pandemic would usher in a Fourth Awakening with an uptick of spiritual curiosity. Considering the history of the Christian church in America, if Keck is right then this would be the beginning of a new era of change in American religion, dramatic and far-reaching in its scope. So far, American historians have identified three Great Awakenings in this country. The first took place in the English colonies in the years between 1730 and 1740 and was characterized by religious revivals and fiery sermons from many pulpits. The Second Great Awakening came soon after in 1795–1835, featuring camp meetings in the towns and larger cities of frontier America. The Third Great Awakening occurred between 1850 and the early 1900s when the missionary movement was born, the YMCA was formed, and several new Protestant denominations got their start. This Third Awakening was characterized by preachers who focused on the social gospel and it ushered in the Chautauqua Movement with summer worship at lakeside retreat centers. If there is a Fourth Great Awakening underway, then churches would do well to consider positioning themselves at the center of this renewal. Religious leaders should be prepared to reimagine the purpose and mission of the congregations they serve, because that kind of awakening ushers in new vitality, but it never comes without a certain amount of disruption.

All the religious leaders we spoke to raised questions about the prospects of institutional religion even as they gave voice to the importance of their work and the gaping holes in our society that their churches filled. The COVID-19 pandemic demonstrated the importance of faith communities in a crisis and the hunger in this nation for social services with a faith perspective. They yearned for wisdom that was greater than despair and for a sense of hope that together people could make it through this crisis and somehow make sense of it.

❁

"The world needs churches like ours," said Rev. Melanie Enfield from Newington, Connecticut, not without some passion. She recalled going to the Connecticut State Legislature to give a prayer. Her church later posted her words on Facebook. "People loved it," she reported. "It can feel like the church has been discarded but people want to hear from us and see us filling this public role." She explained that not long ago she inserted her church into a secular holiday stroll. To everyone's surprise, a thousand people went through her sanctuary, many stopping to pray. Fully twelve hundred viewed their live nativity Christmas presentation, a depiction of Mary and Joseph surrounded by real animals. Because of this pandemic, she said, "It feels like we've raced ahead ten years. We need screens in our sanctuaries and we need to produce videos easily. Though the pandemic pushed us ahead, we're still settling into the newness. There are blessings to this change, and blessings to having to pivot, but now we must keep pivoting and keep adjusting. We must trust God and let God be God. We also must break the shell of the Church because the world needs us. We are the ones who make meaning and bind people together."

❁

With more questions than answers, clergy continue to lead their congregations as the nation emerges from this COVID-19 pandemic. Though the crisis challenged all the people in our survey more than any other event in their career, they persevered. The adversity they faced demanded continual adjustment, pastoral fortitude, and real vision. The crisis required them to be more creative than ever, as they made the perpetual pivots needed to serve the people they cared for so deeply. More than most people in society, clergy are expected to cast a vision and see into the future, if only dimly through faith's eyes. They are the oracles who ask important questions and read the signs of the times. In this moment they have also been under-appreciated for their heroism and pluck, their compassion and courage. Balancing the needs of so many others had long become an occupational skill and in this crisis, the clergy became a force for life, as well as a source of new life.

❊

When asked "Why did God cause this pandemic?" I responded, "God did not cause it, but God's not going to waste it." Rev. Beth Gedert, Delaware, Ohio.

Who We Are

MEET PEGGY

Rev. Peggy O'Connor has eighteen years of experience as an interim pastor working with congregations through times of transition and change. She has also concurrently been a spiritual director in both Lowell and Boston, Massachusetts. Recently she has served as Chaplain Administrator of the United Church of Christ Society at the Chautauqua Institution in New York. Prior to becoming a pastor, Peggy was a psychotherapist in Maine. For our book, she brought her experience as a pastor, spiritual director, and psychotherapist to the interview process. She is fascinated by the similarity and uniqueness of the stories we are hearing as well as the ways this experience has affected clergy.

MEET SUSAN

After forty years as a minister, Susan was part of the Great Resignation and left her position as settled pastor of Pilgrim Congregational Church, UCC in Harwich Port, Massachusetts, in the summer of 2021. Motivated by the unique opportunity to do this research and write about how the pandemic has affected faith leaders, she pivoted from being a full-time pastor to conducting interviews with colleagues. Then in 2022, after there was a draft of this book, she took a position as interim senior pastor at First Congregational in Appleton, Wisconsin. Navigating church life and leading a congregation as the church emerged from this pandemic gave her a chance to live into the questions in this book, which added clarity to the editing process.

Acknowledgements

We feel grateful to have enjoyed the encouragement of many people as we worked on this book. Clergy and church people who heard what we were doing volunteered to participate, to recommend the project to others or to lend their enthusiasm at many points along the way.

We feel fortunate to have been guided and influenced by colleagues who were thoughtful and articulate about how the COVID-19 pandemic changed them and shaped their ministry. Again and again we were inspired by what they told us, by their commitment to the people of God, and by their bedrock faith.

We want to give special thanks to our own pastor Rev. Nell Fields, who understood the idea and proposed that the Barnstable Association of the Southern New England Conference of the United Church of Christ support it officially. Her immediate enthusiasm gave us a boost when this project was in its infancy. We owe a debt of gratitude to Rev. Dr. John Dorhauer, the minister and president of the United Church of Christ who saw the importance of our work and responded with immediate support, which added some wind to our sails.

This book began to germinate on the ample porch of the UCC Society at the heart of the Chautauqua Institution. We conducted the initial interviews there and found many leads for the second round of conversations from among our Chautauqua friends. In the interview process Dr. David Shirey introduced us to Rev. Kim

Gage Ryan, one of the co-directors of the Bethany Fellows who was generous with her time and ideas.

During our writing process we received encouragement from Judy Weintraub, president of Skillbites and Henry Devries, CEO of Indie Books. We are indebted to Judy for believing in this project and to Henry for his initial feedback and the idea for a title.

This book would simply not have become what it is without the editorial advice of Rev. Amy Lignitz Harken who brought her astute writer's eye to every page and recognized the weight and power of these stories. Her appreciation for what we hoped to accomplish and creative suggestions in the writing process helped to make these stories sing.

Finally, we appreciate the families of faith whose stories are told in these pages. They inspire us and help us appreciate how congregations can thrive and soar in good times and bad. Of course, we will always be grateful to our own families and our friends who have become like family, where talk of the church is the bread of life at many tables where we gather.

Susan Cartmell & Peggy O'Connor

List of Clergy Interviewed & The Questions

THESE ARE THE CONGREGATIONS that the clergy served at the time of their interviews. Given the length of the study and the transient quality of ministry during the pandemic and after it, some clergy are no longer serving at these congregations.

Rev. Dawn Adams, Pastor
First Congregational Church, Brimfield, MA

Rev. Dr. Candi Ashenden, Pastor
Athol Congregational Church, Athol, MA

Rev. Loletta Barrett, Pastor
Whittier's First Friends Church, Whittier, CA

Rev. Mary Bauer, Lead Pastor
First English Lutheran Church, Appleton, WI

Rev. Bradley J. Berfalk, Intentional Interim Minister
Hillcrest Covenant Church, Prairie Village, KS (focus of his answers)
Arvada Covenant Church, Arvada, CO

Rev. Dr. James Brewer-Calvert, Senior Pastor
First Christian Church, Disciples of Christ, Decatur, GA

Rev. Dr. Joanne Brown, Pastor retired 12/2020
Des Moines United Methodist Church, Des Moines, WA

Rev. Dr. Randy Bush, Senior Pastor
East Liberty Presbyterian Church, Pittsburgh, PA

Rev. Quinten Chin, Pastor and Chaplain
First Congregational Church of Southampton, Southampton, MA
HospiceCare in the Berkshires

Fr. Greg Christokos, Pastor
Saints Anargyroi Greek Orthodox Church, Marlborough, MA

Rev. Kathleen Clark, Pastor
Federated Church of East Arlington, Arlington, VT

Rev. Paul Davis, Associate Minister
Congregational Church, UCC, Greensboro, NC

Rev. Melanie Enfield, Senior Pastor
Church of Christ, Congregational, Newington, CT

Rev. Nell Fields, Pastor
Waquoit Congregational Church, Waquoit, MA

Rev. Laura Folkwein, Pastor
Pilgrim Congregational, United Church of Christ, Bozeman, MT

Rev. Sue Foster, Pastor
East Woodstock Congregational,
United Church of Christ, Woodstock, CT

List of Clergy Interviewed & The Questions

Rev. Fritz Fowler, Senior Minister
Trinity Evangelical Lutheran Church, Lansdale, PA

Rev. Leah Fowler, Pastor
The Presbyterian Church in Leonia, Leonia, NJ

Rev. Beth Gedart, Pastor
Zion United Church of Christ, Delaware, OH

Rev. Elizabeth Goodman, Pastor
Church on the Hill, UCC, Lenox, MA

Rev. Dr. Robyn Gray, Pastor
First Congregational Church of Washington,
UCC, Washington, CT

Rev. Deb Grohman, Pastor
First Presbyterian Church of Ontario Center, Ontario, NY

Rev. Anna Guillozet, Senior Minister
Linworth United Methodist Church, Columbus, OH

Rev. Brent Gundlah, Pastor
St. Paul United Church of Christ, Navarre,
OH
Holladay United Church of Christ, Salt Lake City,
UT

Rev. Kristen Heiden, Pastor
East Cobb United Methodist Church, Marietta, GA

Rev. Lauran (Laurie) Heidenreich, Pastor
St. Paul's United Church of Christ, Attica, NY

Rev. Julius Jackson, Pastor and Chaplain
Trinity Emmanuel United Presbyterian Church, Rochester, NY
Chaplain St. John's Home, Rochester, NY

Rev. Ellen Jennings, Pastor
Cleveland Park Congregational Church,
United Church of Christ, Washington, DC

Rev. Dr. Jim Keck, Senior Minister
First Plymouth Congregational Church, UCC, Lincoln, NE

Rev. Emily Keller, Senior Pastor
Congregational Church of South Dartmouth, Dartmouth, MA

Rev. Amy Lignitz Harken, Pastor
Mattapoisett Congregational Church, UCC, Mattapoisett, MA

Rev. Lucia Lloyd, Rector
St John's Anglican Church, Bowmanville, ON

Rev. Dr. Jeremy Lopez, Pastor
Salem United Church of Christ, Tonawanda, NY

Rev. Bette McClure, Pastor
First Congregational Church of Fairhaven, Fairhaven, MA

Rev. Rebecca McElfresh, Associate Minister
Church of the Good Shepherd, Sahuarita, AZ

Rev. Loren McGrail, Interim Minister
Irondequoit United Church of Christ, Rochester, NY

Rev. Eileen Morris, Pastor retired 2021
Slatersville Congregational Church, UCC, Slatersville, RI

Rev. Julie Peeples, Senior Minister
Congregational Church, UCC, Greensboro, NC

Rabbi Carl Perkins
Temple Aliyah, Needham, MA

List of Clergy Interviewed & The Questions

Rev. Gordon Pullan, Pastor
North Hadley Congregational Church, North Hadley, MA

Rev. Nico Reijns, Pastor
Girdwood Chapel United Methodist Church, Girdwood, AK

Rev. Nancy Rosas, Pastor
Pilgrim-St. Luke's United Church of Christ, Buffalo, NY

Rev. Dr Ruth Shaver, Interim Pastor
The Congregational Church of Mansfield, UCC, Mansfield, MA

Rev. Nicole Shaw, Paster
First Congregational UCC, Angola, IN

Rev. David Shirey, Senior Minister
Central Christian Church, Lexington, KY

Rev. Ruth Snyder, Pastor
Church of the Nativity, UCC, Tonawanda, NY

Rev. Scott Spencer, Pastor
Woodridge Congregational, UCC, Cranston, RI

Rev Stuart Spencer, Senior Pastor
First Presbyterian Church, Moorestown, NJ

Rev. John Sweet, Pastor
First Presbyterian Church, Brookline, MA

Rev. Pam Werntz, Rector
Emmanuel Episcopal Church, Boston, MA

Rev. Holly Woodruff, Pastor
Seventh Street Christian Church,
Disciples of Christ, Richmond, VA

Rev. Dr. Patrick Wrisley, Senior Pastor
First Presbyterian Church, Fort Lauderdale, FL

QUESTIONS ASKED

Few institutions were changed more than churches in this recent pandemic with all it laid bare about our healthcare and our divisions as a nation. Few people have stepped up as much as the clergy in our churches.

> What was your biggest challenge?
>
> What are you most proud of?
>
> How has the pandemic experience changed the way you lead and how you see your role as a religious leader?
>
> How has the pandemic shaped you as a pastor?

AUTHORS' NOTE

While the above statement and questions were put to each of our interviewees, the material we gathered was far more wide ranging that the questions would indicate. In each interview we both asked follow-up questions after each of the participants answers, seeking clarification and a fuller understanding of the answer. For while the questions sought specific information, the answers were full of emotions that often said far more than the factual answers. For example, when we heard that their biggest challenge was figuring out online worship, we would ask what made it so hard. Their responses to the follow up questions painted a rich and nuanced picture of what it was like for them and the toll it took upon them, to respond to the COVID-19 pandemic and all of the social and racial divides it brought to the surface.

We can never thank our participants enough for their unfailing willingness to be open, introspective, and vulnerable with us.

Bibliography

"2 Year Trends: Pastors Feel More Loneliness and Less Support." Barna, Jul 12, 2023. https://www.barna.com/research/pastor-support-systems/.

"38% of US Pastors Have Thought About Quitting Full-Time Ministry in the Past Year." Barna, Nov 16, 2021. https://www.barna.com/research/pastors-well-being/.

Anderson, M. T. "After a Plague, a Reckoning." *New York Times Opinion*, Feb 20, 2022.

"Attendance at Religious Services." https://www.pewresearch.org/religion/religious-landscape-study/attendance-at-religious-services/.

"Back to Normal? The Mixed Message of Congregational Recovery Coming Out of the Pandemic." https://www.covidreligionresearch.org/wp-content/uploads/2023/09/Epic-4-2.pdf.

Banks, Adelle M. "Churches' Ministry to Those Hurt by the Pandemic Shows 'Monumental' Growth, Study Says." Religion News Service, Dec 21, 2021. https://ministrywatch.com/churches-ministry-to-those-hurt-by-the-pandemic-shows-monumental-growth-study-says/.

Bass, Diana Butler. "Religion After Pandemic: Lost Means Gone—It Also Means Dislocated." *The Cottage*, Apr 26, 2021. https://churchanew.org/blog/posts/diana-butler-bass-religion-after-pandemic.

Beaumont, Susan. "Getting on the Same Page Now." Congregational Consulting Group, Apr 21, 2021. https://congregationalconsulting.org/getting-on-the-same-page-now/.

Beaumont, Susan. *How to Lead When You Don't Know Where You're Going.* Lanham, MD: Rowman & Littlefield, 2019.

Brooks, Geraldine. *Year of Wonders.* New York: Penguin, 2001.

Cotter, Holland. "For Big Museums, It's Time to Change." *New York Times*, Mar 22, 2020.

"Cotton Mather." Wikipedia. https://en.wikipedia.org/wiki/Cotton_Mather.

Douthat, Ross. "Can the Meritocracy Find God?" *New York Times*, Apr 11, 2021.

Bibliography

Dyer, Rob. "They're Not Coming Back." Baptist News Global, Sep 14, 2021. https://baptistnews.com/article/theyre-not-coming-back/.

Elton, Terri. "Ministry in the Pandemic Leader's Survey." faith+lead, Sep 20, 2020. https://faithlead.org/blog/ministry-in-the-pandemic-leaders-survey/.

Grinspan, Jon, and Manseau, Peter. "It's 2086. This Is What American History Could Look Like." *New York Times*, Jan 6, 2022. https://www.nytimes.com/2022/01/06/opinion/jan-6-shaman-past-future.html.

Howard, Barry. "Twelve Trends for Being Church in a Post-Pandemic World." Baptist News Global, Aug 28, 2020. https://baptistnews.com/article/12-trends-for-being-church-in-a-post-pandemic-world/#.YLUse5NKjfZ.

Jones, Jeffrey M. "US Church Attendance Still Lower Than Pre-Pandemic." Jun 26, 2023. https://news.gallup.com/poll/507692/church-attendance-lower-pre-pandemic.aspx.

Kaufman, Julie. "For Some Church-Goers, Singing Hymns in Isolation is Not a Solo Act." WBUR, Apr 12, 2020. https://www.wbur.org/news/2020/04/12/church-goers-hymns-isolation-together-holy-week.

Kirkpatrick, Nathan. "Greeting Our Return When the Old Is Gone and the New Is Here." Faith and Leadership, Apr 6, 2021. https://faithandleadership.com/greeting-our-return-when-the-old-gone-and-the-new-here.

Krisberg, Kim. "COVID-19 Pandemic Fueling Rise in Child Hunger: Malnutrition, Wasting Risks Rise among Youth around World." The Nation's Health, Apr 2021. https://www.thenationshealth.org/content/51/2/21.

Lange-Kubick, Cindy. "Loving Their Neighbors: Church Helps Pay Off Their Medical Debt." *Lincoln Journal Star*, Mar 26, 2022.

Langston, Katie. "Are Digital Communities Church?" *faith+lead*, Jun 2, 2021. https://faithlead.org/blog/are-digital-communities-church/.

Leonhardt, David. "Americans Claim to Attend Church Much More Than They Do." *New York Times*, May 17, 2014.

Lovett, Ian. "Houses of Worship Face Clergy Shortages as Many Resign." *Wall Street Journal*, Feb 21, 2022. https://www.wsj.com/articles/houses-of-worship-face-clergy-shortage-as-many-resign-during-pandemic-11645452000.

Martin, Stephanie. "Barna: What Churchgoers Missed Most About In-Person Services." The Barna Group, Apr 7, 2021. https://www.barna.com/research/churchgoers-miss-services/.

Marty, Peter. "Six Predictions for the Post Pandemic Church." Christian Century, Mar 10, 2021. https://www.christiancentury.org/article/editorpublisher/six-predictions-post-pandemic-church.

McCaulley, Esau. "Why You Can't Meet God Over Zoom." *New York Times*, Dec 27, 2020.

McFee, Marcia. *Think Like a Filmmaker: Sensory-Rich Worship Design for Unforgettable Messages*. Truckee, CA: Trokay, 2016.

Bibliography

"Modeling the Future of Religion in America." Pew Research Center, Sep 13, 2022. https://www.pewresearch.org/religion/2022/09/13/modeling-the-future-of-religion-in-america/.

Morgan, Tony. "Why Church Leaders Can't Afford to Wait and See." Lewis Center for Church Leadership, Feb 8, 2022. https://www.churchleadership.com/leading-ideas/why-church-leaders-cant-afford-to-wait-and-see/.

"Navigating the Pandemic: A First Look at Congregational Responses." Nov 2021. https://www.covidreligionresearch.org/research/national-survey-research/navigating-the-pandemic-a-first-look.

Nienaber, Susan. "From Languishing to Flourishing." Congregational Consulting Group, Jun 1, 2021. https://www.congregationalconsulting.org/from-languishing-to-flourishing/.

"Pastors Share Top Reasons They've Considered Quitting Ministry in the Past Year." Barna, Apr 27, 2022. https://www.barna.com/research/pastors-quitting-ministry/.

Peers, Lawrence. "Resign from Ministry—Or Take a Pause?" Congregational Consulting Group, Feb 21, 2022. https://congregationalconsulting.org/resign-from-ministry-or-take-a-pause/.

Pew Research Center. "Americans Growing Less Religious and More Strictly Religious at the Same Time." https://baptistnews.com/article/americans-growing-less-religious-and-more-strictly-religious-at-the-same-time/.

———. "More Americans Than People in Other Advanced Economies Say COVID-19 Has Strengthened Religious Faith." Pew Research Center, Jan 27, 2021. https://www.pewforum.org/2021/01/27/more-americans-than-people-in-other-advanced-economies-say-covid-19-has-strengthened-religious-faith/.

Poser, Rachel. "The Iconoclast." *New York Times Magazine*, Feb 7, 2021.

Rainer, Thomas. *The Post Quarantine Church: Six Urgent Challenges and Opportunities That Will Determine the Future of Your Congregation.* Amazon Books, 2021

Rice, Sarai. "A Thousand Tiny Changes." Congregational Consulting Group, May 17, 2021. https://congregationalconsulting.org/a-thousand-tiny-changes/.

———. "Play and the Revival of the Church." Congregational Consulting Group, Feb 28, 2022. https://congregationalconsulting.org/play-and-the-revival-of-the-church/.

———. "What Congregations Can Learn from the Pandemic." Congregational Consulting Group, Nov 16, 2020. https://congregationalconsulting.org/what-congregations-can-learn-from-the-pandemic/.

Skjegstad, Joy. "Relationships Are Key in the Post-Covid Church." Building Faith, April 6, 2022, https://buildfaith.org/relationships-are-the-key-in-post-covid-church/.

Tickle, Phyllis. *The Great Emergence*. Grand Rapids: Baker, 2008.

Walker, Andrew T. "Lessons for Streaming Synagogues from the Evangelical Experience." *Mosaic*, Mar 8, 2021.

Bibliography

Wang, Wendy and Elhage, Alysse. "Here's Who Stopped Going to Church During the Pandemic." *Christianity Today,* Jan 20, 2022. https://christianitytoday.com/ct/2022/january-web-only/attendance-decline-covid-pandemic-church.html.

Warren, Rick. "COVID-19 Has Revealed A Fundamental Weakness in the Church." *Christian Post,* Dec 23, 2020. https://www.christianpost.com/news/rick-warren-covid-19-revealed-a-fundamental-weakness-in-the-church.html.

Wertheimer, Jack "How Will Synagogues Survive?" *Mosaic,* Mar 1, 2021.

White, Dr. James Emery. "5 Ways the Pandemic Has Changed the Church." Crosswalk, Jul 1, 2021. https://www.crosswalk.com/blogs/dr-james-emery-white/five-ways-COVID-has-change-the-church.html.

White, Lesli, "Four Ways COVID-19 Has Changed Worship: Is It Time to Reimagine What Worship Looks Like?" Beliefnet. https://www.beliefnet.com/faiths/4-ways-covid-19-has-changed-worship.aspx

Whiting, Dr. Michael. "Pandemics and the Church: What does History Teach us? *Campus News Dallas Baptist University*, March 30, 2020 https://www.dbu.edu/news/2020/03/pandemics-and-the-church-what-does-history-tell-us.html

Wilson, Bill. "Your Church After COVID: Restart, Refresh or Relaunch?" Baptist News Global, July 24, 2020. https://baptistnews.com/article/your-church-after-covid-restart-refresh-or-relaunch/.

Wimberly, John. "Getting Ready." Congregational Consulting Group, Sep 27, 2021. www.congregationalconsulting.org/gettingready/.

———. "Why Stay a Pastor?" Congregational Consulting Group, Nov 7, 2022 www.congreationalconsulting.org/whystayapastor/.

Witvliet, John D., Snyder, Noel, Cornou, Maria, and Jang, Chan Gyu. "Pandemics and Public Worship Throughout History." Calvin Institute of Christian Worship, Mar 23, 2020 https://worship.calvin.edu/resources/resource-libraryj/pandemics-and-public-worship-throughout-history.

Worthen, Molly. "400 Years Ago, They Would Be Witches. Today, They Can Be Your Coach" *The New York Times*, Jun 3, 2022 https://www.nytimes.com/2022/06/03/opinion/spiritual-coaches-religion.html.

York University, "Churches Have a Vital Role to Play in Post Pandemic Recovery" PHYS ORG, May 18, 2021, https://phys.org/news/2021-25-churches-have-a-vital-role-pandemic-recovery.html.

Yount, Steve, "Churches Closed in 1918 Too: Here's What Christians Can Learn Today." The Christian Post, Apr 9, 2020, https://www.christianpost.com/voices/churches-closed-in-1918-too-heres-what-christians-can-learn-today.html